Vagabond
Fever

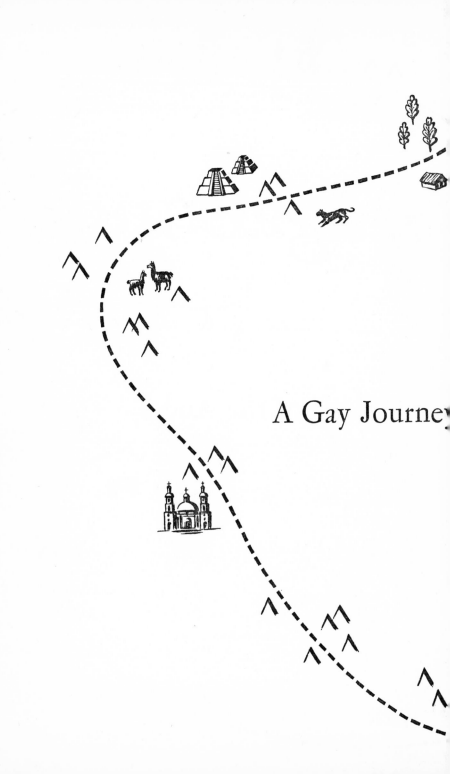

A Gay Journey

Vagabond Fever

n the Land of the Andes

by KARL ESKELUND

RAND McNALLY & COMPANY

Chicago • New York • San Francisco

American Edition Edited and Published by
Rand McNally & Company
Copyright 1954 by Karl Eskelund

Copyright 1953 by Karl Eskelund

Library of Congress Catalog Card Number: 54-8902

First Printing, June, 1954

Printed in the United States of America by Rand McNally & Company

Contents

Contents

List of

Photographs

List of Photographs

Vagabond
Fever

Guatemalan Medley

MEI-MEI SOMETIMES COMES TIPTOEING INTO MY ROOM WHEN I am busy writing, and asks me to play with her. Daddy has to work, I tell her—otherwise we can never get a car. Mei-mei wants a car more than anything else and this explanation usually satisfies her. But one day she was especially bored and begged me to tell her a story. Just one!

"We'll never get a car if ——" I began.

"But, Daddy," she interrupted, "can't you work just a *little* less? And I can get a bicycle instead."

My wife and I realized that what Mei-mei really needed was a playmate. We both felt rather guilty because she is an only child. It isn't easy to have a large family when you travel as much as we do.

Once we thought that Mei-mei had found an answer to the problem, without involving us in the usual complications of having a baby. As far as I remember, it was four or five months after our arrival in Guatemala. I was reading something to Chi-yun, when Mei-mei suddenly appeared at the door and said, "Shhh!"

"What's the matter?" we asked.

"Don't speak so loudly!" she whispered, looking at the heavy, invisible burden she carried in her arms. "You'll awaken Little Sister." Carefully she placed the armful of air on Chi-yun's lap.

Little Sister stayed with us for about two months. She and Mei-mei went for long walks together, gathered flowers, built houses, and got tummy aches from eating green mangoes.

A kitten put a sudden stop to Little Sister's career. Mei-mei saw it in the village one day and immediately found out that it was for sale for ten cents. Wouldn't we please buy it for her? We explained that we might be leaving soon, so it would be unwise to have a pet. And anyway, she had Little Sister to play with, hadn't she?

Mei-mei nodded thoughtfully. When we got home, she took Little Sister by the hand and went down to the lake. Half an hour later she returned alone. Little Sister was dead, she told us—she had fallen from a tree, broken into a thousand pieces, and already been buried; now Mei-mei had no one to play with, but for ten cents . . . . .

I hope my daughter will never again commit murder to have her own way!

She soon regretted the exchange, for the kitten was not nearly so easy to manage as Little Sister had been. It stubbornly refused to go swimming and raised strong objections when Mei-mei pulled its tail. And when we put iodine on the scratches left by its sharp claws, she howled like a pig.

So we had to face the old problem again—with whom was she going to play? We live in an Indian settlement, and our neighbors have clearly shown that they do not care for us. The nearest family is only a stone's throw away; through a mass of coffee-tree leaves we can see their straw-thatched hut. We knew that the family consisted of four: father, mother, daughter, and a newborn baby. Almost every day on our way down to the lake to swim we would pass the mother, the baby hung in a bundle on her back and a big clay water jug balanced on her head. Her blue-and-white-striped cotton skirt reached to the ankles; nut-brown breasts peeped out through two slits in her embroidered blouse. Her features were Asiatic, and if she had worn one of Chi-yun's dresses, she could easily have been mistaken for a Chinese woman.

On seeing us, she would step aside on the narrow path. At first we smiled at her, but she only stared straight ahead while the coffee flies buzzed around her. When we had passed, she would walk on with soft, rolling steps.

Her husband was usually busy in the fields. We did not know for sure how tall he was because he was always kneeling down, working on the neat onion beds. The calluses on his bare feet were as thick as shoe leather.

He could not help seeing us when we went by, but we seemed to interest him no more than the buzzards hopping about. In the early morning they would spread out their wings, wet with dew, to dry them in the sun; from a distance they looked like big fans. I don't think he liked the birds, but he could not stop them from lighting on his land. We had moved into the house next to his, and there was nothing he could do about that either.

Their daughter was perhaps three years older than Mei-mei. I say perhaps, because it isn't easy to guess the age of an Indian. You see a thin girl, a child with frightened eyes, and a few months later you notice that she has become a woman with breasts and hips. People ripen quickly under the Central American sun, even up on the rather cool highland where we live.

The daughter would disappear into the thicket as soon as she saw us, her long plaits sticking straight out from her head as she ran. How Mei-mei succeeded in breaking the ice I never discovered, because at that time she knew only a few words of Spanish; but somehow those two found each other. Mango, as the little girl was called, had a restraining influence on Mei-mei, and we appreciated it. She was quiet and demure, almost unnaturally so for a child. She spoke in a low, whispering voice and never got excited. For hours she would squat, watching with her doe-like eyes while Mei-mei built houses or cooked food of earth and leaves. That Mango took only an inactive part in the games did not worry our daughter, who plays the star part herself and appreciates a silent spectator.

Our neighbors continued to ignore us despite the friendship between the two children, till one day Mango had a toothache. My father, who is a retired dentist, pulled out the bad tooth. Next morning we received a large basket of onions and oranges from Mango's father. Eager to cement the fragile acquaintance, we sent Mei-mei over to them with a present of an almost new oil lamp.

From now on they would greet us whenever we met. Mango's father rose from his knees and doffed his straw hat; he was taller than we had expected. The mother only showed her white teeth in a shy smile. Mango no longer ran off when my father or I approached the spot where she and Mei-mei were playing.

One day, about a month after the tooth-pulling, Mei-mei did not come home, although it was past her dinnertime. Chi-yun became anxious and asked me to go and find her. I went to our neighbors' house without, I admit, any real reason for looking for her there—but I was curious to see how they lived.

Only the mother was at home, kneeling in a corner of the rather large room. There were no windows, and my eyes had to adjust themselves to the semidarkness before I could make out that she was grinding corn for tortilla dough in a stone trough. In one corner of the earthen floor lay a pile of rough-woolen blankets: the family bedstead. In another, there was a primitive fireplace made of large stones. Soot had blackened the ceiling, and there were no tables or chairs, only an unplaned, unpainted wooden chest. On a crossbeam stood the oil lamp which I had given them. It was covered with a thick layer of dust.

Mango's mother stopped her work and looked at me. Had she seen Mei-mei? She shook her head. Not knowing what else to say, I pointed at the oil lamp.

"Don't you use it?" I asked.

She put a fresh handful of corn in the trough.

"It's a good lamp," she said slowly, "but we have our candles—we are used to them."

During the following months we occasionally stopped and discussed the weather with our neighbors. They answered very politely, and once my father pulled out a tooth for the mother. We felt we knew them fairly well.

Before Christmas they threw a big party. There were more than a dozen guests, and they had a three-man marimba orchestra. Shortly after sunset we decided to visit our neighbors and wish them a Merry Christmas. They had lighted a lot of candles outside the hut, and their guests were jumping about in a circle while the orchestra banged away. It was a strange dance—the women stamped their feet in time with the monotonous tune, while the men flapped their arms up and down and uttered blood-curdling howls.

The moment they saw us the orchestra stopped playing. The dancers halted, too, and a man who had been busy emptying a bottle of firewater let his arm drop. In the sudden silence Mango's father came toward us. He was not quite steady on his legs.

"Buenas noches," he said. Our own voices sounded unnatural when we answered. There was an oppressive air of hostility, and later Chi-yun and my father told me that they had felt it too.

"This is a fiesta for Indians," said one of the guests after a silence of several seconds.

We beat a hasty retreat, and as soon as we were out of the garden, the orchestra started again. After going to bed, we lay for a long time listening to the noise and laughter. Why had they treated us like that? What did they have against us?

When you live among the Indians, you often ask yourself such questions. It is almost impossible for a foreigner to understand their way of thinking, and by "foreigner" I mean all non-Indians. Sometimes they make you furious, as happened one day when Chi-yun and I went for a walk through the village. About halfway we passed an Indian boy sitting by the roadside and holding a rope tied round a cow's neck.

The animal was grazing peacefully enough, but suddenly it turned and rushed at Chi-yun. She could easily have been gored by the sharp horns, but fortunately was caught right between them, hurled up in the air, and landed none too gently on her back.

The boy watched the performance with great interest, and not until it was over did he pull the animal away.

"She always does that," he said. "She's a malicious cow."

The Indians will laugh loud and long when one of them walks under an avocado tree and is hit by a falling fruit. It hurts the victim, but he laughs even more uproariously than the others. Or, if some poor wretch is pursued by a swarm of bees, the others are greatly amused. But tell them a really good joke, and they just look blankly at you.

In the village across the river there is a little movie theater. It has no walls and the straw roof leaks, so it is wise to keep away during the rainy season. The Indians occupy the front seats and are usually much more entertaining than the movie. If it is a comedy, they follow the action with dead seriousness. A tear-wringing lovers' drama will bring on peals of laughter. Why? I don't know.

At the village market we sometimes see them quarreling among themselves. They will gesticulate a little with one hand, but even when the squabble reaches its climax, they never raise their voices. One gets the impression that they are making plans for a funeral. So far as I know there's only one thing which upsets them—if a woman steps over their goods spread out on the ground in the market, they'll grunt and push her away. When you bargain with them, they will stare blankly and absent-mindedly; and you have to repeat every word at least twice before they deign to understand. If you offer them a lower price, they will either nod casually or yawn and glance elsewhere, which means they don't want to sell.

The Indians are small of stature, but tough. When there is a market in a neighboring village, they will walk from ten to twenty miles with a burden of close to two hundred pounds. They carry the goods in large wooden frames hung on their backs, the frame supported by a broad leather strap across the forehead.

One day I saw a whole mountain of wooden furniture move down the path outside our garden. There were four chairs, two tables, a chest of drawers—and underneath it all, a perspiring Indian. We needed some new furniture—when we had guests for bridge we had to sit on the ground —so I stopped him and asked where he was going. To a village five miles away, he said; there was to be a market next day, and he hoped to sell the furniture. How much did he expect to get for it? About five dollars.

"I'd like to buy it," I said. "I'll pay you five dollars, and you'll save yourself the walk."

"That's true enough," he answered. "But if I do that, I'll miss the market." He wiped his forehead and staggered on.

The Indians are stupid, people say, but I'm not so sure. Once I listened to a conversation between an elderly Indian and an American philologist. The American was interested in the grammatical construction of the Quiche language; among other things, he wanted to know how the Indians expressed the passive tense and the possessive form.

At once they encountered difficulties. The Indian in-sisted that the passive form did not exist in Quiche.

"That's impossible," said the American. "You just don't get what I'm driving at. Let's do it slowly—let's say, for instance, that you have a house. You have one, haven't you? Good. Now, let's assume that your house can talk and that it says, 'I have been built.' How would you express that in Quiche?"

The Indian shook his head. "A house which can talk!" he exclaimed. "Perhaps that exists in your country, *Señor,* but our houses never say anything."

"O.K., O.K.," said the American. "Let's forget that for a while." And then he concentrated on trying to find out how the Indians used a possessive pronoun. The Indian didn't seem to understand, so he pointed upward.

"The sky," he said. The Indian nodded and repeated the word in Quiche. "Now, say *my* sky."

"How can I?" protested the Indian. "After all, the sky belongs to all of us, doesn't it?"

The American sighed and thought for a moment. "You know the word for lice?" he asked. Again the Indian nodded. "Can you say *my* lice?"

The Indian rose with dignity.

"I suppose we all have our troubles with lice," he said. "But *we* prefer not to speak of such things."

Even a promise of twenty-five cents could not make him resume the conversation.

The Indians are actually not very interested in money. An acquaintance of mine, a foreigner, has a fairly good business exporting embroideries to the States. Once a week he is visited by an elderly Indian couple who sell him twenty embroidered napkins. One day he received a large order for just that type of napkin. So the next time they came, he asked them to make twice as many napkins.

"If you want more napkins than usual," they said after a moment's hesitation, "you'll have to raise the price."

"But, why?" asked the businessman. "That doesn't make sense. On the contrary, you should *lower* the price for a larger order."

"That may be the way you look at it," the Indians replied quietly, "but we earn enough as it is. Why should we work any more than we need?"

About half an hour's walk from our bungalow lies a tourist hotel. Some years ago the owner wanted to enlarge it, so he sent for his Indian neighbor and offered to buy his land. First he suggested three hundred dollars. It was a fair price, but the Indian refused point-blank. He doubled the price, trebled it, and finally lost patience. "All right," he shouted, "I'll pay you fifteen hundred dollars."

Still the answer was no.

"But fifteen hundred dollars is more than you can earn in a lifetime," the man said. "Think what you could do with so much money—you could build a new house and buy twenty times as much land as you have now."

"Perhaps," the Indian replied, "but the land has belonged to my ancestors for many hundreds of years. They wouldn't like it if I sold it, and what could I do with twenty times as much land? I have enough already. And why should I build a new house? I like the old one."

The land and their ancestors mean a lot to the Indians. Are they Christians? The Guatemalan Government says so, and they certainly go to church. God's house stands empty during the week, but early on Sunday morning it becomes a lively place. The cool stone hall is illuminated by hundreds of flickering candles, and a gentle murmur rises from the crowd of kneeling Indians. They don't exactly pray to the saints, however—they bargain with them.

"You give me a good harvest," they will say, "and I will buy six fine wax candles for you. But then you'd better stop being so stingy with the rain. The fields are thirsty, and remember that you got flowers and a corncake last Sunday. If you don't send a couple of showers, I won't give you any more candles and . . . . ."

The wife and children squat patiently in the background while the father talks to the higher beings. When he has finished, they bring the sacrifices. Invariably they make a pretty pattern of pine needles, flowers, and corn on the floor before the altar.

Then they go to a lonely spot in the mountains to pray to an ancient Mayan idol. On leaving the church, they pass the witch doctors who stand on the very steps of the holy building, performing their magic rites over flaming fires. The Indians have a much deeper respect for these men than for the Christian priests. A witch doctor doesn't waste time bleating in an unknown language, nor does he talk about how wonderful everything will be in the next world if only one contributes generously to the church. No, the witch doctor is more realistic—he swings his staff which has a piece of cloth tied to one end. Can you feel the air blowing against your face? That was the breath of the gods. Then he shakes a long metal chain which he always carries—it is the footsteps of the gods you are hearing!

Have you an enemy? Tell the witch doctor about it; he

will see to it that the scoundrel gets the punishment he deserves. From his capacious cloth bag he will produce a small wax figure and hold it over the fire while he mutters sinister incantations. It represents your enemy. Shall we push a needle through his stomach? Then, of course, he will get a bad stomach-ache, but perhaps that's too humane a punishment? All right, then we will pierce his head. Now he will have a terrible headache and may even go mad. What about a sprained ankle or a broken arm? We can also do away with him entirely, but that takes longer and costs more money. Or we can burn salt while we mutter his name, or bury bones or a cross under his doorstep. The Indians have great respect for the cross. It is an ancient Mayan symbol and originally stood for the four corners of the world and the concept of life.

The witch doctor does not only maintain connection with evil forces; he can also make pious wishes come true. If the patient has confidence in him, he can chase malignant spirits out of the body or cure sickness. But do not ask him what his medicine is made of. If you do, he will become offended and return the money. That is *his* secret. He always has a bottle of firewater on hand, for the work is strenuous and he and the gods need a little refreshment from time to time. First the witch doctor takes a mouthful and spits it out into the fire. That is for the gods. Then he takes a big gulp for himself. He never cheats.

Chi-yun and I went on a two-day walking trip when we had spent about a year in Guatemala. High up in the mountains we came to a village inhabited only by Indians. The magistrate, an elderly man with a red-woolen cloth wrapped around his head, received us in a friendly manner.

We were the first foreigners he had seen for a month, he said; the Spanish priest came only at Christmas and at Easter to say Mass.

He showed us round the church. There was not much to see apart from the usual saints, but in a small side room we discovered a strange statue of a bearded man wearing a ragged foreign suit. A cigar hung from his mouth, and he was smiling devilishly with smug self-satisfaction. In one hand he held a bottle of liquor; in the other, a pack of playing cards.

"Is that also a saint?" we asked.

"Not really."

The magistrate smiled awkwardly and explained that it was an old superstition. There used to be similar statues in most of the villages. When the priests arrived, they were always carefully hidden, however, for the statue represented the Spaniards and the half-breeds. Later I discovered that the original name was "The Lord Who Is Bound." In the olden days it was sometimes carried along in the religious processions of the Indians. Their children were encouraged to spit at it as a kind of bogy.

As I stood there looking at the hideous figure, I began to understand many things—why Mango's parents preferred their homemade candles to our oil lamp, why they had practically driven us away from their party, why the Indian would not sell his land to the hotelkeeper. It seemed to me that a red thread ran through all these acts, and it led straight back to the statue of "The Lord Who Is Bound."

The Lord
Who Is Bound

"THE LORD WHO IS BOUND" ARRIVED IN THE YEAR 1523—A bearded young Spaniard riding at the head of 435 white soldiers. The Indians called him "Son of the Sun" because of his flaming red hair. His name was Pedro de Alvarado.

Alvarado was brave and strong. He was also greedy and utterly ruthless. It would have been difficult to find a better soldier or a worse administrator.

With his handful of men he conquered a country about the size of New York State. It is believed that Guatemala at that time had about half a million inhabitants; they were descended from the Mayas who, a thousand years before, for unknown reasons, had left their great cities near the Mexican border and wandered north and south. Those who went south settled down on the Guatemalan highland and later split into separate tribes which were constantly at war with each other.

If they had united against the "Son of the Sun," they

24

might have been able to stop him. But.they did not, and he subdued them one by one. Their chiefs and priests were burned, their temples destroyed, and the people were divided among the Spaniards as slaves.

The white soldiers had brought only a few women along. Celibacy did not appeal to them, and during the first few decades after the conquest many children were born whose skin and hair were *café au lait* in color. The Spaniards usually took the half-caste girls for their mistresses, so the half-caste men were forced to marry Indians. They multiplied rapidly, and for a time it looked as if the Indians would eventually disappear, absorbed by the new mixed population.

It was the witch doctors who prevented this. They had fled into the mountains when the Indian armies were beaten. From their hide outs in holy caves they followed the tragic developments. The white man had taken their country, and now he threatened to destroy their race. How could it be prevented? Magic spells did not help: the Spaniards seemed immune to them. Therefore the solution must lie with the Indians themselves. They had to be stopped from mixing with the foreigners. "The Lord Who Is Bound" was probably the product of a clever witch doctor's imagination. He introduced him as a new god, and the Catholic fathers had already paved the way for him by telling the people about the devil. Here he was in person!

The Indians did not worship this new god. They hated and despised him. He became the symbol of one of the most successful underground resistance movements in history. No use to puncture him with needles, the witch doctors explained. He was as powerful as he was evil. But you could be on your guard against him, and pity the poor Indian who was not! Many a young girl was put quietly out of the way because she succumbed to the advances of a Spaniard or a half-caste. If it was not her fault—if the man had taken her by force—the newborn child was made to pay for the sin of its father.

The witch doctors went one step further. It was not only the white man's blood which must be fought. Everything connected with him was declared taboo for the Indians. They must not dress like him, talk like him, or use the modern implements which he had introduced.

Only the religion of the white man was accepted by the witch doctors, at least in part. It was clear that the foreign gods were powerful. They deserved respect. It was useless to forbid the Indians to go to church. They were forced to. Why fight the inevitable? The wise old men undoubtedly realized that the walls of the churches were stronger than their own foreheads, so they compromised. The heavens were large, they said—there was ample space for both the old and the new gods. An Indian could go to church with a clear conscience, provided that he paid a visit afterward to one of the venerable stone statues which stood, and still stand, in remote places in the mountains. The idea appealed to the Indian. He felt safer than before—if the old gods would not aid him, surely the new ones would.

The holiest statue in Guatemala is the "Black Christ" at Esquipulas. Tens of thousands of Indian pilgrims kneel before him each year. He does not belong to the race which subdued them; maybe he puts in an especially kind word for them when he talks to his Father.

The "Dance of the Conquistadors" is performed once

a year. It has a strong religious significance and gives the impression that the Indians admire their oppressors. Men disguised as Spanish soldiers fight great battles with native warriors, and the spectators always clap when the latter succumb.

But that does not mean that the Indians have become fond of the whites. It was a strong serum which the witch doctors injected some four hundred years ago. It still works. If a vain Indian buys a fancy jacket of foreign cut, the village elders will put him in a corner with orders to keep out of sight until he is decently dressed. If an Indian girl is seen with a half-caste, her parents will kick her out of the house and no Indian will have anything to do with her. They respect the Spaniards for their strength and courage, but they still hate them.

During the last few decades the authorities in Guatemala have begun to realize that they can never change their country into a modern nation without the help of the Indian. Everything is now being done to win him over. He is a free man. In many cases the land which was taken away from his forefathers has been given back to him. His children can go to school without payment; they can even get university education for nothing. He can choose any career he likes. Practically all doors are open to him.

But the Indian refuses to be modernized. For four centuries he had to fight to preserve his customs and his own way of life. And throughout those four hundred long, hard years he was a despised slave. He emerged from this purgatory a strong, dignified individual. The Guatemalan Indians are the only inhabitants of the New World who were conquered and yet remained intact as a people. The country today has a population of nearly three million. A little more than half of them are full-blooded Indians. Some of them have given up their old costumes, but only for economic reasons. A homespun, embroidered shirt costs more than three times as much as a factory product. One hardly ever sees "The Lord Who Is Bound" any more, but the Indians have not forgotten him. To them he is still the representative of evil forces—of the white man and the half-breeds.

The white man wants schools, railroads, and bridges. The Indians ask, what for? All they want is to be left in peace. They have accepted the white man's God, but not his priests. In many villages the Indians will not permit a Catholic priest to be present during their religious ceremonies. They marry without his blessings, die without his comforting words. Patiently they till the fields with the same crude implements used by their forefathers. They grow their corn and beans just as they have always done, and carry heavy burdens over the mountains as if the motorcar had never been invented. Our mechanical wonders are no temptation to them. They prefer their own simple, frugal way of life. I think that if Christ came down to earth again, he would feel far more at home among the Indians than in one of our modern cities.

"The Lord Who Is Bound" is, in my opinion, a rather crude caricature of the half-breeds or "Ladinos" as they are called here in Guatemala. The word literally means "Latins." Both the Indians and the few thousand inhabitants who are pure white look down on the Ladinos—not entirely without reason. They are, by and large, not very trustworthy. Their moral ideas are far from being over-developed. Most Ladino girls become pregnant before they are fifteen, and a large number of Ladinos find it hard to distinguish between yours and mine. We have lost many things since we came here. Once, when we were down by the lake, a couple of Ladinos broke into our bedroom and made off with twenty dollars in silver coins. We sent for the local constable, also a Ladino. He sniffed about the house for a while, and then declared that we had only ourselves to blame for the theft.

"How's that?" we asked.

"People oughtn't to have so much money," he answered.

I know many Ladinos who are charming, intelligent, and excellent drinking companions. But to make them keep a date is virtually impossible, and even if they come from good homes, they do not seem to have learned that honesty is the best policy. They are prodigious liars. I have heard a Ladino boast that he sold his father's cattle to get money for a mistress when he was aged fourteen. He may for once have been telling the truth.

When you talk to Ladinos, they take every opportunity to emphasize that they are of pure Spanish extraction. "His grandfather was an Indian," they will whisper if they want to slander a countryman. An innocently critical remark about Guatemala will make them jump up. Their Latin honor has been insulted!

About a mile from our bungalow lives a German family, and once when we were visiting them, the conversation turned to the Ladinos. The man of the house banged the table. "All Ladinos are useless——" he declared.

"No, they aren't," interrupted a small voice. We all turned to look at Mei-mei.

29

"I am a Ladino," she continued. "And I'm . . . . ."

She stopped, embarrassed by our glances, but her meaning was clear enough—you aren't necessarily a useless scoundrel because you are a half-breed. Chi-yun and I felt proud of Mei-mei. We knew that she was right, but we often wondered why the mixtures here in Guatemala had developed so poorly. Was it due to historical circumstances? Or did Spanish and Indian blood mix badly?

Only many months later did we find the answer—in South America. Not that we went down there to study racial problems. No, we went because I received a letter from New York—a letter that chased us out of the Garden of Eden.

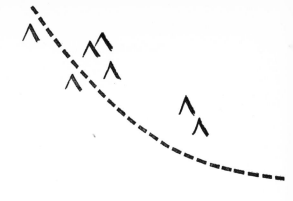

Mei-mei

"The Garden of Eden," is what we call our home in Guatemala, and we love it—the garden where the roses bloom all the year round, the straw-thatched bungalow which looks like a Hawaiian hut, the "Little House"——

Especially the "Little House." I have been in the mansions of millionaires, in the finest hotels which London and New York can offer, but nowhere have I seen a toilet which can compete with ours. It is inspiring. A brook babbles beneath the seat. Above your head, palms wave softly. During the day you can see the blue sky through the foliage; at night the Southern Cross appears, sparkling above the dark mountains. You can sit there by the hour and dream. What does the lack of a door matter? If anyone approaches, the dry leaves on the path always crackle a warning.

The path leads to the kitchen where my father is usually busy at the smoky brick stove. A few years ago he was one of the best-dressed men in Shanghai; now he never wears anything but an undershirt and a pair of faded dungarees. He shaves twice a week—that is, if the lake behaves.

For the lake is our bathtub—the blue Lago de Atitlan, which lies like a sapphire in the middle of the Guatemalan Plateau. It is fifteen miles long, nearly as wide, and no one knows how deep. When we wash ourselves, we can see our faces in the water beside the reflection of two majestic volcanoes. We have no need to worry about how to remove the calluses from our feet, for pumice stones lie thick along the shore. After a heavy rain the lake is speckled with the floating, white stones dug out of the mountain valleys by the rushing torrents.

Father has never learned to swim, and he is suspicious of high waves. When the north wind chases away the lake's placid smile and makes it foam angrily, father will postpone his shave until a quieter day. Sometimes the north wind blows for two weeks at a time.

Chi-yun really ought to do the cooking, but any contact with fire or steel is peculiarly dangerous for her. She has an amazing talent for cutting her fingers, spilling boiling soup over her feet (and remember, we often go barefoot), and covering her face and body with soot. Food cooked by her would taste fine if it were not burned to a cinder, which it usually is.

Once I told her the story of the three Canadian wood-cutters, and now she sometimes looks slyly at me when I complain of her cooking. Those three men lived in a deep forest. They all hated cooking, so they drew lots. The loser had only one consolation: if anyone complained, he had to take over.

The food got worse and worse, but the two others went on eating it. One day the cook swore that he had had enough, and for dinner that night he baked a pie of deer dung. When he served it with chocolate frosting, one of the men took a big mouthful. His face stiffened.

"My God, it's dung!" he shouted, then quickly added in a small voice, "but it's good!"

My father was not nearly so cunning as that woodcutter. He took pity on Chi-yun, or maybe he got tired of eating burned food. Anyway, he became our cook. I'll never forget the first time *he* did the cooking. He wanted to make a coconut cake, but we had no grater, so my father chopped up the nut with his pocketknife. Then he added flour, oil, and mashed bananas, and finally fried the greasy mess over a quick fire.

I took a spoonful, tasted it, immediately muttered, "Excuse me," and ran behind the nearest tree. Chi-yun joined me a moment later. Mei-mei was not nearly so polite; she spat it out under the table.

Father is a stubborn man; he swallowed two mouthfuls. Then he smiled wanly and said, "Maybe it isn't as good as it could be." Shortly afterward he tried to dispose of the remains of the cake by giving it to an Indian boy who came to have a tooth pulled out. Father's Spanish is not very good, but he managed to explain that the cake was supposed to be eaten. Obediently the lad stuffed a handful into his mouth and chewed.

"There you are—he likes it!" said Father proudly, and went to get the syringe and forceps. When he returned, the boy had disappeared, but the cake was still there.

So Father put it out for the neighbors' skinny dogs which

are always hanging about the bungalow stealing whatever they can get. But they didn't deign even to sniff at the cake. Next morning there were traces of rats in the kitchen. They had eaten half a cake of soap, but Father's coconut cake had been left strictly alone.

After this fiasco—perhaps because of it—Father quickly developed into a good if rather unpredictable cook. When there are any leftovers, he invariably puts them into the sauce, regardless of whether it is pea soup or liver paste. To consult a cookbook is beneath him, so we always await his meals somewhat anxiously. Sometimes we have to eat his mashed potatoes with a spoon; sometimes we have to cut them with a knife.

His speciality is a refreshing salad made of avocado pears, garlic, and tomato juice. The district around our bungalow is full of tall avocado trees, and whenever a "plump" sounds, Father and Mei-mei dash out to retrieve the fallen fruit. The buzzards also like avocados, and feathers fly when the old man and the child, armed with sticks, fight it out with the black birds.

Our whole family lives on about sixty dollars a month, everything included, so we naturally do not have much money left over for buying any kitchen utensils. Our entire outfit consists of a few clay pots, a frying pan, five clay bowls, a Finnish boy-scout knife, two forks, three pairs of chopsticks, and half-a-dozen spoons which Father has made out of bamboo and coconut shells. We eat at a stone table in the garden and hurl gnawed bones and crab shells over the shoulder. Mei-mei's table manners leave much to be desired, but one cannot blame her for that—she only copies her parents.

There is a wealth of oranges, lemons, and papayas in the garden. Strawberries we can buy at seven or eight cents a pound from the Indians. Sugar is seldom used in our kitchen: honey is so cheap in Guatemala.

One morning, when I was eating my oatmeal, I complained at the unusual number of ants in the honeypot.

"Be a man!" said Chi-yun contemptuously. "As if a few ants would do you any harm. Eat them—they're good for you."

Next morning I saw Mei-mei sitting at the foot of an anthill, very busy.

"What are you doing?" I asked.

"Eating ants—they tickle the tongue, but Mother says they're good for you."

Mei-mei's upbringing has been left more or less in the hands of my father. In the beginning I was a little skeptical of his methods, for he doesn't believe in corporal punishment.

But Mei-mei and my father get along very well together. Sometimes it makes me feel quite envious, because she obviously respects him much more than she does me. I think his secret lies in the fact that he is never condescending. They talk about everything between heaven and earth; and he never tires of answering her endless stream of questions. When there is something she is not allowed to do, he carefully explains why. If he has to punish her occasionally, he does so by not telling her a bedtime story. Mei-mei would rather have a couple of spankings than miss one of Farfar's fairy tales.

For a while he told her mostly about gnomes and witches. They became so real to Mei-mei that she became scared of going alone to the toilet at night—behind every tree wicked beings lay in wait for her. So Father carved her a wooden knife and told her that so long as she had it with her, even the most evil witch would not dare to do her any harm.

From now on she was no longer scared of the dark: she trusted the witch knife as firmly as she trusts Farfar. One evening she suddenly decided to spend the night with some friends who live about twenty minutes' walk away. She knew the road, she said, and could easily find her way. We put her toothbrush and pajamas in a bag, kissed her good night, and let her go.

A few minutes later I went out to see how she was getting on. It was so dark that I had to feel my way along the path. When I had gone a short distance, I saw two figures standing motionless, watching a smaller figure close by.

Mei-mei had not seen me; her glance was glued to the two Indian women. Suddenly she began to back away from them, and backed right into me.

"Daddy!" she cried, hugging my leg. "Daddy, I think they're witches—I'm going home to get my witch knife."

After the witch stories there was an endless serial about a little girl named Marie Petersen. Marie had the most extraordinary adventures. She was turned into a butterfly, an ant, and a cat. (This was how Mei-mei learned that animals don't like to be maltreated.) She also traveled on all five continents and visited distant lands. Thanks to her, Mei-mei has more knowledge of geography and natural history than I had when I was her age.

Sometimes she puts her father and mother to shame. One

evening we were sitting in the garden looking at the glittering heavenly bodies.

"That must be Jupiter," I said, pointing at a dazzling spot.

"I think it's Venus," said Chi-yun.

"No!" interrupted Mei-mei, shaking her head firmly. "It's Mars." And it was.

Her first birthday in Guatemala was a big event. At that time we had been living beside the lake for nearly a year. Father baked a wonderful cake for her—without coconut—and Mei-mei was thrilled when he brought it in with the candles alight.

"May I blow them out?" she asked with shining eyes.

"Yes," Farfar replied, "but first you must wish—what do you want more than anything else in the world?"

"To blow out the candles," whispered Mei-mei.

Now that she was six years old she had to go to school, at least when the river permitted—a brook which swells to a broad river after heavy rain lies between us and the main village. We were a little nervous about how the other children would receive her. Even here in Guatemala she looks a bit outlandish, and Mango had taught her more Indian than Spanish.

The language difficulties did not bother her much; after two weeks she was talking Spanish in her sleep. But she was teased at first. We noticed that she was silent and depressed when she came home from school, and finally my father asked her what was the matter.

"The other children make fun of me," she replied, tears gathering in her brown eyes. "They call me *Cheena.*"

"*Cheena?* What does that mean?"

"Chinese."

"But you shouldn't mind that!" said Father, taking her on his lap. "On the contrary, you should feel proud of it. Don't you understand—the other children envy you, that's all! None of them has a Chinese mother, I'm sure. Did I ever tell you that Marie Petersen also has a Chinese mother? Oh, I should have—listen to this . . . . ."

Mei-mei was smiling when she came home the following day. She had asked the other children whether any of them had a Chinese mother. They had to admit that none of them had.

"And you haven't got a Danish father either," Mei-mei had continued. "I have, and he has a typewriter."

She must have taken their breath away, for since then the other children have treated her with the respect due to so distinguished a person.

We are never bored here by the lake—I have my work, Chi-yun reads a great deal, and my father pulls out teeth and carves lovely figures out of wood. One of them, a dancing girl made from the root of a tree, he sold to a tourist for fifty dollars. When we tire of each other's company, we only have to go to Panajachel, the village, where a colorful little international group has settled down. There are three painters, two writers, and a couple of sculptors and amateur photographers. You can tell right away that they are artists, because they wear sandals and the men have beards. If you feel like getting tipsy, one of them is always willing to drink with you.

The strangest of all our artistic friends were a young Dutch couple, Jan and Lis. They both had straw-colored hair, blue eyes, and regular, almost noble features; but there was something cold in their manner. At parties they could be lively and entertaining, yet you always felt it cost them an effort. They never revealed their feelings; it was impossible to be on intimate terms with them.

Jan wrote articles and took pictures for European magazines. His main interest was wild animals. Their house was full of slimy reptiles from the coast—snakes of all sizes, baby crocodiles, giant lizards. The first time we dined at their place they served fried rattlesnake with butter sauce. It tasted fine. After the meal Jan entertained us by teasing a poisonous snake. We turned pale, for he held it with his bare hands, but Lis sat unconcerned and played with a little honeybear.

Although we protested, Jan would show off his snakes whenever we visited them. I think he actually got a thrill out of risking his life. He loved to let the boa constrictors curl up his arms and tighten their grip till his veins seemed about to burst. To tease the fer-de-lance gave him the greatest pleasure of all, perhaps because it was more dangerous than the other snakes. He would blow at it, pull its tail, slap it; and every time it struck at him, a smile would appear on his handsome face.

One day it got him. You could hardly see the little hole between the thumb and index finger, but both Lis and Jan must have known what it meant. They said so long to us, seemingly unconcerned, and motored to the capital; no serum was to be had anywhere else.

Lis returned without him. Later I spoke to the people in whose house she lived during the first few days after his death. She never shed a tear, they said. Half an hour after he had died she came to their place and ate a tremendous breakfast.

Several months passed before Lis went back to Holland. In the meanwhile she moved into a hotel by the lake. One afternoon I happened to walk past her room and heard the sound of sobbing through the half-open door. I stopped and glanced in. Lis had not seen me. She was sitting on the bed, crying as if her heart would break. On her lap lay the little honeybear, dead.

Five or six times a month Chi-yun and I go to the hotel and dance for hours to the music of the marimba orchestra. The visiting tourists sit like hawks, waiting for the local characters to turn up. I have no beard and therefore don't count as an artist, but then I have a Chinese wife, and that's almost as good. They're always very kind and insist on treating us. When the bill comes, they snatch it away, and Chi-yun says that I am suspiciously slow at such times. The truth is, I hate violence. Once I did succeed in getting hold of the bill, and the tourists fell upon me and tore it out of my hands. Why should I take such risks again?

Mei-mei sometimes acts as a guide for the tourists. One day she took a couple from Baltimore across the lake and escorted them through the village. They passed a shop, and the man asked her to go inside and see if there was anything worth buying.

"No," said Mei-mei when she returned, "they've got nothing but beer and Jesus Christs." She was referring to the aspirin advertisements, always adorned with a picture of the Savior.

Life by the lake also has its dark side. For instance, there are the niguas [chigoes], little parasites which burrow into your toes and lay their eggs. When they're about to hatch, the places itch unbearably. Personally I like scratching them,

40

and always wait as long as possible before asking my father to cut the skin and remove the little bag of eggs.

About a year ago I met a Swedish scientist visiting Guatemala who wanted to take a nigua nest back to Sweden. He succeeded in getting an excellent specimen to breed in his big toe, but the trip was a long one. By the time he was halfway, he had nearly laughed and scratched himself to death. Later he wrote and told me that he had been forced to remove the niguas three days before he arrived home.

Our bungalow lies about half an hour's walk from the village, and shopping is sometimes a problem. In the dry season we can easily wade across the river, but during the rains we often have to strip partly—that is to say, I have to. Both Chi-yun and Mei-mei are scared of the strong current, so I have to carry them across—first my wife, then my daughter. On the return journey I have to cross the river five times, because then I have also to carry the market basket with a week's supplies. Once I felt lazy and took Mei-mei under one arm, the basket under the other, and Chi-yun on my back. It was not very successful—halfway across I stumbled, had to let go of Chi-yun, and throw myself into the swirling current to save our child from drowning. We never saw the basket again and Chi-yun was furious.

Mei-mei's schooling is also a worry to us. How bad it is we had not realized until two sweet, old American ladies came to visit us one afternoon. Mei-mei had put on shoes and a pretty dress in honor of the occasion.

What a darling child, the two ladies declared. How did she like Guatemala? Okay. Did she like going to school? It wasn't too bad. Did she learn much?

"No," replied Mei-mei, "but I get a lot of lice."

I am afraid she shocked our guests, and we could not even deny her words. Chi-yun has spent hours pulling lice eggs out of her hair, but she always gets re-infected from her playmates. Now we spray her with DDT before she goes to school in the morning; it's the only thing that helps.

Most of the pupils are Ladinos, and in some ways the school is surprisingly progressive. The authorities are eager to raise a healthy generation, so once a day the children are given cod-liver oil.

Some weeks ago Mei-mei began talking about wanting a spoon to take to school with her. I didn't listen very carefully, but she became more and more insistent.

"What do you want it for?" I finally asked.

"To take cod-liver oil," she answered. "All the other children use the same spoon."

Sometimes we long for a change in our rather monotonous diet. Then our thoughts turn to salted herring and strong cheese. Once I wrote to my relatives in Denmark, asking them to send us some anchovies and Roquefort.

The customs office is very strict here in Guatemala. They keep all parcels from abroad for about two months before they inform the recipients of their arrival, and when you go to fetch them at the customs building in the capital, you have to wait for hours, fill in countless forms, and pay outrageous duties.

Imagine our amazement when we received a *cable* informing us that a parcel had arrived for us! I went to town to get it, and this time there was no waiting. As soon as I told them my name, one of the customs officers hurriedly unhooked a parcel suspended from the ceiling.

"Don't I have to fill in any papers?" I asked.

"No," he replied as he almost hurled the parcel at me. "And no duty either, so long as you take it away at once!"

On the way home the other passengers in the bus kept glancing suspiciously at me. To dull my own sense of smell, I smoked many cigarettes. When we opened the parcel, the cheese virtually crawled across the table; but it was delicious and Father and I ate it, worms and all. The anchovies we had to throw away, and during the following days we heard many explosions from the dunghill behind the house.

On our arrival in Guatemala I had begun to write a book about my father. When I had finished it, I decided to take a long holiday, but a few days later I got an inspiration. It came to me in the middle of the night—I suddenly sat up in bed and said, "Chi-yun, I have a wonderful idea for a book!"

She did not even bother to answer. I lit a candle—we have no electricity—and began writing in my notebook. Every minute the idea got better. The setting for the book was to be two cities which I knew well: Shanghai and Chungking. The main character was a young girl whose problems I also knew fairly well: her mother was a Chinese, her father a Dane.

I must have burned half-a-dozen candles that night. When the gray daylight peeped in through our window, I fell asleep, but I dreamed of the book and went on with it when I awoke a few hours later, now working on the typewriter. The metal letters hammered like a boxer's fists. I wrote chapter one, crumpled it up, and began all over again. At lunchtime the floor looked like the bottom of a wastepaper basket. The jump from journalist to novelist seemed much larger than I had ever realized. Hitherto I had only written about people I knew. Now I had to create the characters—create them and blow life into them. They had a terrible tendency to talk endlessly; I could not make them shut up, and they just would not eat or drink or behave like normal human beings.

First I tried writing in Danish. It did not work too well —I have not spoken my mother tongue for ten years, and I had to resort constantly to an English-Danish dictionary. I changed to English, but that was just as bad—I had never learned it properly, and the trite journalistic phrases which I had picked up as a correspondent for a news agency were not suitable for a novel intended to be a literary masterpiece.

Sometimes I wrote twenty pages a day. At other times I would sit from morning to night staring at the same blank sheet of paper. Those were the worst days. When completely stuck, I would hold my nose and empty a couple of glasses of *aguardiente*. Next morning I could write again. This cure seldom fails me: it is as if the hang-over knocks all the complexes out of my head. Or maybe the alcohol clears the brain.

Twice I was on the point of giving up, but it seemed unfair to leave my characters in the lurch—by now I had involved them in many problems, and they would probably haunt me forever if I didn't find a way out for them.

Five or six ribbons were worn to shreds; stacks of paper were devoured by the typewriter. I got calluses on my finger-tips. Greta was the name of my heroine, and Chi-yun said that I was in love with her. I must admit that I found her

44

extremely attractive, but then I did spend most of my time in bed with her—I always sit up in bed when I am writing.

It was Christmas time when I first became interested in Greta. The summer rain was falling in sheets the day I made the final full stop and left her to her fate. The manuscript was air mailed to New York; another copy I sent to my Danish publishers. And then I waited. Most of the time I spent by the lake, gazing at the volcanoes without seeing them: my thoughts were with Greta in New York.

The sun is warm in Guatemala. It shines every day of the year, and you can get dark brown in a couple of weeks. I was nearly black when the answer finally came.

It was an oblong envelope. With shaking hands I tore it open.

Away—
Anywhere!

THE BOOK IS WELL WRITTEN . . . . . EVERYBODY HAS PRAISED
it . . . . . But the poor book market . . . . . Lack of interest
in the Eurasian problem . . . . . Sincerely yours . . . . .

"They don't want it."

I tried to smile at Chi-yun; I was close to tears. For
the first time in my life I had received a rejection slip.

The letter was to work as a much needed kick—it
brought me down to earth. But that day I was not able
to look at it like that. I abandoned myself to despair.
"You're finished," I said to myself. "You can't write." I
refused to talk or to eat, and only really serious things
can make me do that. Toward evening, however, a couple
of friends came and asked us to an improvised beach party
in the moonlight. They had two bottles of whiskey, so I
accepted at once. It was about eight o'clock when we went
down to the lake. At half-past eight they probably regretted
having invited me. One bottle was empty and I was drunk.

At noon the next day I woke up. The purge had had its usual sobering effect on me. I could see myself very clearly. "You're just a newspaper man," I said. "Forget about novels. You can't create—you can only copy. Go out on a trip and get some fresh impressions."

Chi-yun came in to comfort me. Did I want an aspirin? Don't take it so hard, she said. The book is all right; the American publishers just don't know what's good. Maybe I could rewrite the first few chapters, give them more punch . . . . .

I jumped out of bed.

"No, I'm not going to do it!" I exclaimed. "I'll never touch that book again. Chi-yun, I . . . . . I . . . . ." I could see her face change; she hates it when I become dramatic. "I can't stand it—I just have to go away," I concluded.

"Easy now, easy!" She patted my back. This was nothing new—at least twice a year I can't stand it any more, and regardless of our whereabouts I declare that we must go somewhere else. "Lie down, Karl—you'll get over it," she added gently.

"Not this time. Really, I just have to go away—I want you to come along, of course."

"And Mei-mei?"

I felt a stab of pain. "We can't take her along—we're going on a long trip. Father probably won't mind looking after her while we're away——"

"Long trips cost money," Chi-yun said dryly, and this time her objection struck home. Many people seem to think that a writer must be rich just because one of his books has sold well. If I got *all* the money which my books bring in, I should probably be tolerably well off. But, unfortunately, there are two greedy gentlemen who satisfy their appetites before I reach the trough—my agent and the income-tax collector.

My agent takes a bite of everything I earn. If I as much as find a cent, he would like to take his percentage. The income-tax man is even worse, especially in England. Once I received an encouraging letter in which my British agent informed me that my first book had netted so many pounds sterling. I licked my chops: it looked as if the amount would be sufficient to keep us going for a year or two.

Two weeks later the final account arrived: a sad message. The British Government had put half the amount into its own pocket, and another fat slice had gone to the agent. The enclosed check proved barely enough to keep us in cigarettes for a year.

Another time my agent wrote happily that he had sold the book in France for what seemed a fabulous sum—I think it was 42,000 francs ($120). He ended by asking whether I would like a trip to Paris, for it was impossible to take the money out of France.

I wrote to the French publisher and asked him to spend the entire amount on perfume and air mail it to me in Guatemala. My wife's birthday wasn't far away, and perfume seemed the ideal present for her. The parcel did arrive in time, but I became a little suspicious when they sent for me from the village post office. Why had the perfume passed through the customs without any trouble?

When I mounted the post-office stairs, I sniffed—the air had an exotic fragrance. A moment later I was handed a large package. It smelled like a cosmetics shop after a major earthquake, and it rattled.

Chi-yun had no birthday present that year, but Mei-mei's schoolmates were very pleased—they received French air-mail stamps for a total value of 1,700 francs ($4.86).

But there I was in bed with a hang-over, insisting on going away. I would try to get enough money somehow, I told Chi-yun—I would write to Denmark and ask for advances on the articles and the book which I intended to write about the trip.

"But where are we going?" she interrupted.

"I don't know for sure—maybe Africa, maybe the South Sea Islands—wouldn't you like to go to the South Sea Islands?"

"I'd prefer Africa," she said, "but it will probably be too expensive."

Chi-yun is most unromantic, I sometimes think. But without her brutal realism I would probably end in a debtors' prison. It soon proved that she was right: the tickets alone to Egypt would cost close to seven hundred dollars each. Even if I obtained liberal advances, we would hardly be able to go any farther than Ethiopia, and I doubt whether Danes can live on the dole in Addis Ababa.

So we looked at a map of the world and tried to eliminate all the impossible places. It was a heart-wringing process. All the countries which I longed to visit—Java, New Guinea, Madagascar, the South Sea Islands—were prohibitively far away.

"There's nothing left but South America," Chi-yun said at last.

I hung my head. For some strange reason South America had never interested me. People who had been there talked only of Buenos Aires or Rio—*so* like New York or Chicago, they would say, and I hardly considered that much of a recommendation.

Chi-yun bought a guidebook and ordered me to increase my meager knowledge of South America. With many yawns I read about hotel prices, museums, and Spanish architecture. Then I got a little further into the book, and my eyes began racing over the pages. Ruined Inca cities, Negro tribes living exactly like their forefathers in Africa, head-hunters, cannibals . . . . . I asked Chi-yun to borrow more books on South America for me.

Our preparations for the trip did not take long. We pulled out our old leather suitcase from under the bed and scraped off its furry coat of mildew. Fat moths fluttered from our woolen underwear which we had not worn since our arrival in Guatemala. Now we were going to climb the icy peaks of the Andes; so we got busy with needle and thread. Then we made two cunning belts with secret pockets for hiding our money. Then we were ready—all we lacked was the money to hide in the belts.

It arrived at last—two thousand dollars! At the same time we received an air-mail letter from my Danish publisher. He had read the novel about Greta. "Well put together," he wrote. "Exciting . . . . . The main characters are clearly drawn . . . . ." And all these praises weren't just written to take the sting out of a "but." There were no "buts." He wanted to publish the book.

Chi-yun sighed with relief before she congratulated me. She had never quite reconciled herself to the thought of leaving Mei-mei for so many months.

"We shan't be leaving then, I suppose," she went on. "You'll be too busy translating the book, won't you?"

"Oh, no!" I retorted. "Do you think I'm going to miss the Jibaros or the Colorados or Machu Picchu? You have no idea how interesting those countries down along the Pacific coast are—it would be foolish not to go."

"Only two weeks ago you thought South America boring," said Chi-yun with a mischievous gleam in her eyes. "Even if you've forgotten that, what about the novel?"

"Greta can wait," I said. "We're leaving tomorrow."

We spent the rest of the day with Mei-mei. She couldn't understand why her father and mother kept looking at her so sadly.

Gold or Silver

We met Bill and Joan on the plane en route to Panamá. They were Americans, young, newly married, and now they were going out to see the world, the world of 1948.

They were prepared for the worst. The doctor had given them injections against four or five different diseases. A travel bureau had reserved rooms for them at the best "American-type" hotels. They had also brought along two bottles of vitamin capsules and a supply of germ-killing pills for purifying their drinking water.

Bill wore two wrist watches. One of them might fail on the trip, and he could hardly imagine a worse disaster than not knowing the time. Their two-week round trip was measured out to the last minute. They were proud of their itinerary which consisted of five typed sheets: "14.05, arrive Cartegena, Colombia. Two-hour round trip to museums and Spanish forts; 17.05, continue to Cali, Colombia. Sightseeing and overnight stay at Grand Hotel; 7.25, continue by plane to Quito, Ecuador. Three-hour round trip to churches and museums . . . . ."

Twelve days later we met Bill and Joan outside the airport in Bogotá. Now they had seen all South America. Bill gave us a quick résumé of the high lights of the trip.

"We were delayed for three hours in Lima," he said, "and three-quarters of an hour at Antofagasta, so we missed Machu Picchu. Be sure not to go to the Royal Hotel in Santiago—the mattresses were so hard we couldn't sleep a wink. Rio was terribly hot, and Joan got dysentery at Viña del Mar. But that was her own fault; she insisted on eating raw fruit despite my warnings. What place did we like the best? Buenos Aires! Boy, wait till you get your teeth into those two-inch steaks!"

Bill glanced at his wrist watches. "Afraid we have to run," he added hurriedly. "The plane leaves in twelve minutes, and we haven't even had time to buy a post card of Bogotá yet . . . . ."

"We've been so busy writing post cards that we've hardly had time to see anything," added Joan. "Have a good trip . . . . ."

We are not such highly organized—or such thoroughly immunized—travelers as Bill and Joan. They will probably never get typhoid, but then they miss the wonderful sickness which makes our temperatures soar every time we start on a trip: travel fever.

Flying is doubtless the best remedy against travel fever. At least it always cures me. On the way to the airfield in Guatemala City I was shaking with excitement. We boarded the plane and at once my fever began to go down. I can quite understand that bombing pilots can kill a few hundred people and then return to their base and eat a hearty breakfast of bacon and eggs. Up there you feel completely cut off from the rest of the world. The landscape whose outlines are discernible far down below is of no more interest than the moon, and who wants to look at that for long?

During the next four hours we visited as many countries. I could have learned far more about them by sitting at home in the rocking chair and reading a geography. We could see the clouds, the sea, an endless brown mountain chain with green spots here and there, and nothing else. The airports where we made short stops were as interesting as small-town railway stations. San Salvador was the only place which distinguished itself in any way; we could buy beer there instead of the inevitable Coca Cola.

It was dusk when the plane landed for the fifth time. We knew little about Panamá except what we had read in the guidebook. I remembered only two sentences: "Visit Panamá, most international city in the world . . . . . Enjoy modern comforts in the metropolis where North, South, East, and West meet and blend in perfect harmony . . . . ."

At first it looked as if the guidebook had not exaggerated. From the airport we took a taxi down the main street, and in the gathering darkness the city reminded us of Shanghai. Neon lights shone, cars honked, and in the crowds along the sidewalks you saw the blond hair of the Northern European, the dark, greasy locks of the Latins, yellow faces with broad cheekbones, black faces with thick lips.

Then the taxi turned a corner and we drove down a narrow alley. A mob of naked Negro children were shrilly pursuing a rag ball. The stench was worse than that from a garbage dump.

"Here's a reasonable place," said the driver, pointing toward a dim entrance. Street urchins had made rude drawings on the signboard advertising room and board. Outside the door stood a full garbage pail.

"It looks a bit dark——" I began.

The driver jerked himself round to face me. "So the gentleman don't like dark people?" he snarled. "Ain't that too bad! You ask me to take you to a cheap place, don't you? Well, you find no cheap places except in the colored district."

"My husband only meant that the entrance looked dark," Chi-yun put in.

"Oh." The driver, a mulatto, did not sound really convinced. Reluctantly he agreed to take us to another place. He stopped in an alley which did not smell quite so bad. Chi-yun stayed in the car while I walked up a steep, creaking staircase. Ring Three Times for Landlady, said a notice on the door. I rang three times. When I leaned against the wall, my perspiration left a dark spot. The humid heat was almost unbearable.

The door was opened and a fat Negro woman stared at me. "No vacant rooms," she snapped. Whether it was true or not, I don't know, but I think she enjoyed banging the door in my face. We tried another place; another door was banged. Finally we had to go to a fairly nice and not very cheap hotel where they gave us a room. After a cold shower we went down to the dining room. Most of the guests had brownish complexions and only a little kink in the hair. We could feel their glances as we walked to our table. The conversation, lively when we entered, continued in low voices. It reminded me of going into Mango's parents' garden to wish our neighbors a Merry Christmas. These people also instinctively disliked us, and it was because I was white.

We soon understood why the Negroes in Panamá are not fond of the whites. The day after our arrival we met a very hospitable American couple who took us for a ride through the Canal Zone. We were impressed by what we saw—the Yankees have transformed their tropical strip of Panamanian territory into a little piece of "God's Own Country." We ate ice cream in their air-conditioned clubs, visited great food centers where you could buy vegetables flown in from the States. It was hard to believe that at one time this was the most dreaded pesthole in the world. There isn't a mosquito now, and according to a popular story a small boy from Panamá was amazed when he saw a fly on his first visit to the United States. "Daddy, isn't that a *tiny* hummingbird?" he exclaimed.

The Americans brought cleanliness and efficiency to Panamá, but—unfortunately—their racial prejudices, too. The first time I wanted to go to a public toilet, I was startled to see two doors. "Gold" it said on one; "silver" on the other.

"What does that mean?" I asked a friend.

" 'Gold' is for whites," he answered as if it were the most natural thing in the world—of course a white man could not urinate in the same place as a "nigger"!

The entire Canal Zone is divided into "gold" and "silver." The difference between the two sections is about the same as between a nice residential district and a slum in an American town. The terms came into use many years ago, when Negro workers there were paid in silver, the whites in gold.

Now they all get paper money, but the abyss between the two races still exists.

Recently the terms "gold" and "silver" were forbidden, but not segregation. The Americans avoid all contacts with the Negroes. When they speak to them, something commanding creeps into their voices. "Yessir!" the Negro says, but his eyes are resentful.

Our American friends also drove us through the residential district on the outskirts of Panamá. Along the shady boulevards lay palatial mansions surrounded by green parks and high walls. Here live the rich Panamanians—the people whose names are in the local Blue Book. To enter their doors, one must have almost pure Spanish blood. Even white North Americans aren't good enough: they consider the Yankees vulgar and have as little to do with them as possible.

"Snobs!" the Americans say—but most of them could not say it in Spanish, for they have not learned the language.

We visited the market which lies close to the harbor. The great hall was seething with people; we had to use our elbows and step carefully to avoid slipping on banana skins and other refuse. Cooks and housewives of the lower classes rushed from booth to booth with big baskets on their heads, feeling cabbages, weighing mangoes in their hands, sniffing at bloody meat. Prices were shouted in the hot air.

In one corner sat four Indians—small, brown jungle people who had come to the city on some errand. They wore short pants made of crude, homespun cotton, and their straight black hair fell over their naked chests. The noise and the stench didn't seem to bother them, and they took no notice of the city dwellers rushing past them.

No one knows for sure how many Indians there are in Panamá. The Spaniards, when they invaded the country, tried to make slaves of them; but the primitive natives took to the jungle. Since then they have fought so valiantly for their freedom that there are still large areas where no white man has ever set foot—poisoned arrows command a certain respect, for in the jungle they are more effective than machine guns.

Chi-yun and I were invited to several cocktail parties in the American Zone, and at one of them we met Joe, a portly, jovial union boss who immediately slapped me on the back and called me Karl. I listened eagerly while he talked about his union's program—he wanted the zone administration to pass a law guaranteeing equal pay for Negro and white workers.

"You'll never get that law through," someone remarked.

"It's got to go through," replied Joe. " 'Equal pay for equal work' is our motto, and we'll fight for it."

A little later I asked him whether there were many Negroes in his union. None, he answered. That puzzled me. Why then did he worry so much about the Negro wages? But I admired him. Most Americans are democratic so long as you leave the Negroes out of the picture, but Joe seemed consistent in his idealism.

Toward midnight the party went to a private night club. On arrival at the entrance Joe stopped and looked uncertainly at me. I was in my shirt sleeves.

"I'm afraid that won't do," he said. "Wait a minute."

He went inside and borrowed a crumpled jacket from the hat-check girl.

"We're kind of stuffy," he said with a broad smile. "Have

to wear a jacket, and you won't ever see us admit anyone who has even a drop of Negro blood—don't want any niggers here."

I was so amazed I couldn't say anything. Where was my idealist? When we sat down, I asked another man in the party about Joe. He was from the Southern States, I was told, and would like to see all Negroes shipped back to Africa. But why, then, did he want to secure better wages for them?

The man laughed.

"Politics," he said. "Joe is scared of unemployment among the members of his union, so he's trying to make some new, well-paid jobs for them. First he gets the salaries of the Negroes raised, then he tries to get the Negroes kicked out, and then his own boys step in and take over the good jobs. Good old Joe, he's a smart egg!"

Next day we left for Colombia. As the plane rose, I could recognize the different places we had visited—the Negro slums, the residential district of the Panamanian aristocrats, the neat American Zone and behind it all, the jungle. I thought of the guidebook's phrase, "The metropolis where North, South, East, and West meet and blend in perfect harmony"—and I could not help smiling.

Not a
Bad Business!

BARRANQUILLA, COLOMBIA'S MAIN PORT, IS NOT A PLEASANT place during the dry season. Dust whirled across the flat, desolate fields as we drove from the airport. Dust hung in the oppressive air and burned our nostrils. We sat with tightly shut eyes and lips, almost knocked out by the heat and the blinding light.

On approaching the town, we awoke from our stupor—the stench worked like smelling salts. There are no garbage collectors on the outskirts of Barranquilla, nor any drainpipes. Along the road stood wretched hovels made of rough boards, clay, and corrugated iron. I caught a glimpse of a ragged woman who emerged from one of the huts, crawled down to a ditch, and filled a pot with water. A few feet away a boy was urinating into the same ditch.

The houses were crowded close together. Dark-skinned people with bright clothes moved in the narrow patches of shade along the sidewalks. Choking gasoline fumes overpowered all the other stenches. Cars rushed down the street which divided and then encircled a small park that had no flowers or shrubs, only a statue of some Spanish hero. This was the center of the town.

"Pension Victoria," we said to the driver. Chi-yun had found the name in our guidebook under "Hotels"—the best places were marked with two stars, the second-best with one, but poor little Victoria had no decorations at all. That was why we had chosen it, and it did prove cheap; a double room with bath and full board for $1.20 apiece. The food was not uneatable; it was only difficult to swallow the first mouthful—after that you couldn't taste anything. The Colombians like to spice their food with a yellowish powder so strong that it immediately paralyzes your sense of taste.

The dessert looked like a bird's droppings. When I took a spoonful and tried to raise it toward my mouth, I lifted the plate too. It was as sticky as glue and tasted like syrup extract, but we felt obliged to eat it because the waiter had just told us that it was Colombia's national dessert, and he stood close by watching us with an expectant smile.

"Call me at dinnertime," I said to Chi-yun after lunch; I had an article to write. It became a long article, because in Colombia as elsewhere in South America dinner is not served until nine o'clock. Society people dine at about midnight and go to bed about two or three in the morning. One wonders how they can possibly reach their offices at 8:00 A.M. when the working day starts, but after lunch they take a siesta for two hours and thus catch up on their lost sleep.

At ten o'clock we had finished eating and went outside. Three smartly dressed Negroes rushed toward us and offered to exchange dollars at nearly twice the official rate. Some barefoot boys assured us that we would not look decent until we had our shoes shined. A mulatto woman with pleading eyes had shoelaces and pocket combs for sale, and a young taxi driver promised to show us all the wickedness of the world if we would only step inside his rickety, old car.

He won—we had heard so much about the wild night life of South America and were curious to see it. I agreed to pay him the equivalent of a dollar for a return trip to the amusement district some miles from the city. Chi-yun was a little doubtful about the situation—perhaps the girls would resent her presence. Not at all, I told her. Girls of that type are seldom enthusiastic about their work; they long for a husband and a home and like the company of "nice" women, for it gives them a feeling of respectability.

As we drove along the bumpy road, the street lights seemed as far apart as milestones. Here and there a candle flickered behind a window. Hundreds of people lay sleeping on the sidewalk, and every time a car passed they were enveloped in dense clouds of dust.

And many cars passed: the men of Barranquilla were rushing to the red-light district. Most of them probably had wives and children at home, but in Latin America it is considered quite natural for a married man to keep a mistress or—if he cannot afford one—to go to brothels. Men of all classes are unfaithful to their wives, and many illegitimate children are born. South America is truly a man's world, for a wife is seldom allowed to go out alone. Upper-class women have servants, but the great majority of the female population must scrub and cook and give birth to countless children. No wonder they often look like old hags before they're forty.

I had always thought that Japan had relatively more public girls than any other country, but some of the South American nations must surpass it. In Barranquilla, a city of less than three hundred thousand inhabitants, there is a district of two square miles where every second or third building is a house of prostitution.

"The cabarets are over there," said the chauffeur when we got out of the car. "And if you turn left at the second street you'll come to—uh—the cheaper district."

I took Chi-yun's hand, for two men had approached and were staring critically at her. They were in their shirt sleeves and smelled of raw alcohol; it can be bought anywhere in Colombia for about sixty cents a quart.

"Let's get away from them," Chi-yun whispered. But we could not hurry because the road was full of stones and deep holes. The two men walked toward a woman standing under the nearest street light. She was barefoot and carried a child in her arms. The men said something to her. She began to answer, but broke into a cough. They laughed stupidly and walked on.

Hot jazz blared from the cabarets. We looked inside two of them; through thick clouds of tobacco smoke we could see the girls sitting with their legs apart, their short skirts pulled almost up to their hips. A few couples were dancing—drunken men who pawed their partners as they staggered around. On the orchestra stands perspiring Negroes blew on saxophones or hammered away at big bass drums.

We went inside one place and ordered beer. It was a

large cabaret with about twenty girls and a phonograph which was started as soon as the orchestra took a rest. The young ladies—some of them couldn't have been over fifteen —looked curiously at Chi-yun. Two of them had Negro blood, and they seemed more popular than the others.

"How do you do!"

A short lady, elegantly dressed and almost without make-up, stood beside our table. She smiled at Chi-yun.

"May I sit down? I'm the owner, and I am very pleased to have you here." She spoke English with the charming accent of the Spaniards. "Perhaps you will permit me to treat you to a drink. I see that you are having beer. Wouldn't you prefer sherry?"

Mrs. Morrison, our hostess, called a waiter and ordered a bottle. While we waited for it, she told us that she was married to an American engineer.

"You are surprised to see me here?" She smiled again, showing very pretty teeth. "My husband is in the jungle most of the time, you see, and I had nothing to do while he was away. So I said to myself, 'Why not go into business?'"

She lowered her voice.

"And this is not a bad business, you know. I earn as much as my husband. Of course, it isn't good for my reputation among my friends in the city; but never mind, we shan't be here long. As soon as we have enough money, we shall go to the States and settle down in California. I have been there and like it so much. Have you any children?"

Mrs. Morrison had two, and now she and Chi-yun began showing each other photographs and talking about children. At the bar some men started a quarrel, broke a glass, and were kicked out by the drummer, a heavyweight, who also served as bouncer. Every few minutes the conversation was interrupted by one of the girls, who came over, handed Mrs. Morrison some money, and was given a key.

".... I love children—what did you say, Mr. Eskelund? No, I don't mind telling you about my business, not at all! Upstairs I have six rooms which I let by the hour. They are usually"—she searched for the right word—"they are usually occupied all night long. Besides that, my girls pay me a small sum for permission to work here. I allow them to sleep in the room during the day, and sometimes to bring their children here—most of them have children boarding outside. This is a picture of my boy. It was taken the day before he went to the States . . . . ."

We drank three glasses of sherry. Mrs. Morrison wouldn't let me pay for it.

"It was such a pleasure," she said. "Good night, and thank you for coming."

The night air outside seemed very cool and pleasant. We walked toward what the driver had described as the "cheaper district." In the doorways stood half-naked girls, shouting invitations to passing males. Behind them, above the dirty beds, we could see candles burning before colored pictures of saints. Prices were bandied about—three pesos—no, that was too much, one peso . . . . .

Suddenly we heard a siren and began to run—a police car was coming! It stopped with screaming brakes, the girls shrieked—not with fright, but with joy, for the constables jumped off and disappeared inside the huts. We could hear their voices through the open doors; the constables got cut rates.

Chi-yun said that she had seen enough, so we returned

to the taxi. About a hundred feet away from it stood the barefoot woman whom we had seen earlier in the evening. She still had the child in her arms, but when she saw a man approaching, she put it on the ground and walked toward him. She said something. He shook his head. Then she grabbed his arm and her voice became imploring, but he tore himself away. The woman went back to the child, gently picked it up, and returned to the street light to wait for the next chance. We heard her cough, and then the engine started and we drove away.

Magdalena's
Muddy Waters

To THE NORTH AND WEST THE HOT SHORES OF COLOMBIA ARE washed by the Atlantic and the Pacific; to the south and east lie the Andes and the wet jungle of the Amazon. If you want to reach the heart of the country—the Colombian highland—you must go by plane or sail up the river. It is also possible to drive, but we heard disquieting reports of people who had left Barranquilla a fortnight before and had not yet arrived at their destination—Bogotá, the capital. The Colombian roads are fond of playing tricks on drivers; they often dive below rivers or hide beneath landslides.

The river route is quite safe—in most places the water is so low that you would have to lie down in order to drown yourself. All the same you need ample stores of patience and canned goods, for the Andes frequently turn off the water supply. Then all traffic comes to a standstill on the Magdalena, Colombia's main trade route; the Bogotanians must do without oranges and bananas from the lowland, and the inhabitants of the coast cannot enjoy any of the capital's industrial products. Meanwhile, the cargo boats are stuck in the mud, and sometimes a fortnight or even a month passes before the water rises.

We were lucky. A few days before our arrival it had rained in the mountains on the border of Ecuador, so the Magdalena was flush when we boarded the river boat in Barranquilla. The yellow water gurgled happily and all the ships were about to weigh anchor.

Did I say ships? They looked more like floating sandwiches, these broad, clumsy, paddle steamers. Ours had three decks, and on the lowest one heat waves from the furnace hit us in the face. We hurried up the stairs, but halfway I stopped. I had not quite realized that human beings lived on the burning deck we were leaving so hastily. Now I looked down on them—more than a hundred people, packed so close together that many had no room to lie down. Mothers sat with children on their knees, perspiration streaming down their bodies; men wearing nothing but underpants were dipping clay pots in the river, hoisting them up and drinking greedily. Their backs looked like washboards as they leaned over the side, and every time they drew a breath it seemed as though their ribs would break through the skin.

I found myself trying to avoid the dark eyes staring at me. I could not force my own to meet them, for they seemed to cry: What right have you to live in luxury upstairs while we are being fried down here? And I had no answer.

On the deck above it was relatively cool; whirling electric fans set the clammy air in motion and most of the passengers had already refreshed themselves at the bar. Well-dressed and well-fed men and women reclined in comfortable lounge chairs along the rail. Two priests in long, white robes promenaded, deep in conversation. A young man in a striped suit was persuading a giggling girl to smoke a cigarette.

Another stairway, and we were on the top deck: the luxury section. Americans would have found much to complain about, but by Colombian standards it was "de luxe." The captain stepped forward and introduced himself; he had polished fingernails, and he would neither sit down nor lean against the rail for fear of soiling his neat white uniform. We met the other passengers; they had Spanish names and smart Spanish mannerisms. Waiters served ice-cold lemonade and set up bridge tables.

When the sun set, we were many miles from the dirt and noise of Barranquilla. The trees of the jungle bent over the banks, birds twittered, and curious crocodiles raised their heads above the muddy water. The paddle wheel turned slowly, and at the prow stood a sailor who sounded the water with a long stick. Soon he was only a shadow against the rosy evening sky.

At that moment a phonograph on the first-class deck abruptly interrupted our reveries. Colombian music will make the hair of the uninitiated stand on end. It sounds as if the musicians of a circus band have quarreled, and each one is playing a different tune. The crooner screams at the top of his voice to drown the noise and sometimes breaks into violent sobs of despair.

I felt inclined to do the same, for the phonograph played nonstop until three or four in the morning, night in, night out. A marathon dance was in progress in the first class. I believe that several of the couples would have had excellent chances in international competitions, because they knew how to save their strength—only their backsides swayed while they danced, their feet were never lifted from the deck.

Some of the girls smoked as they shuffled around. Their lips must have been honey-sweet: Colombian cigarettes are rolled in paper which has been dipped in a sugar solution. It was interesting to watch them, for whenever they took a puff they would put the *burning* end of the cigarette into their mouths! Many uneducated Latin women smoke in this way; it is hard to imagine why they think it "smart," but they do.

The South Americans speak enthusiastically of the beauty of the Magdalena, but personally I find the Missouri much more interesting as a river—at least it has some variety. The Magdalena is like a beautiful but infinitely boring woman: once you have had her in your arms, she ceases to attract you. But you cannot get away from the river —day after day you see the same green jungle, the same muddy water; and in the end you grow to hate her.

The ports are as monotonous as the river: small clearings in the jungle with about two-dozen, corrugated-iron sheds, a church, and an entertainment district. At night the sailors go ashore to have fun with the girls, whose ragged offspring, meanwhile, climb on board the ship and steal everything that is not locked up or nailed down.

You see practically only Negroes and mestizos in these ports. The real inhabitants of the jungle—the Indians— keep far away from the towns. There are several tribes, and some of them remain as unknown as the Neanderthal man.

The wildest of them all live close to the Venezuelan border; scientists consider them among the most primitive people in the world. You hear many fantastic stories about them: They are said to have tails and to be hairy like apes. Then some of them are reported to be white, the supposed descendants of a German expedition which disappeared into the jungle nearly a century ago.

Only one thing is known for certain about these Indians: they stink. Oilmen and gold diggers claim that you can smell them at a distance of fifty feet. "Then you throw yourself down and start shooting blindly to frighten them," they say. "Probably a spear or an arrow will come flying, and if it hits a bone you might as well write your last testament. The arrowhead is made of brittle palm wood which splinters inside the wound; even with the aid of a microscope you couldn't get them all out."

Some years ago two children—a boy and a girl—were captured by an oil expedition. As far as could be judged they were eight or nine years old. They were stark naked and bit and scratched like wildcats until they were put into a wooden box. Their language consisted of hoarse, animal-like sounds. There was an airstrip close by, and they were to be flown to the capital the next morning; but when the box was opened, both children were dead—they had bitten through their own arteries at the wrists.

As we penetrated farther inland, the jungle became less dense. In some places there were large clearings, and here the grass grew as tall as a man. It is said that the Magdalena Valley could be made sufficiently fertile to feed millions of cattle. But the Colombians don't like the heat; more than two-thirds of the ten million inhabitants live in the highlands and leave the jungle, which covers more than 75 per cent of the country, to a few hundred thousand Indians.

The days crept by. The paddle wheel dug up the mud from the river bottom, for the Rain Gods had taken another holiday, and in some places the water was less than three feet deep. When we got stuck, it took several hours to maneuver the ship into a deeper channel. Then the mosquitoes came in dense swarms from the jungle and attacked the half-naked bodies on the lower deck. In the first class the phonograph roared, and up on our deck the passengers began yawning over their cards. The trip had become rather boring by now—even bridge ceases to interest if you have too much of it.

On the ninth day, the test of patience was over. We hurriedly left the ship to buy tickets for the train going to Bogotá. Two of the passengers from the bottom deck had to be carried ashore, but I don't think our companions in "first" and "luxury" noticed it—they were too busy making plans for their visit to the capital.

Bogotá was the most beautiful capital we visited on our trip, but also the one we liked least.

It lies in a valley about 8,700 feet above sea level, surrounded by copper-colored mountains on whose highest summit stands a white statue of Christ, arms raised toward the sky. The air is thin and cool and makes one think of a sunny, frosty day. Green fields encircle the city which has a population of more than half a million. The streets are broad and clean, and in the shadow of the modern steel buildings lie idyllic houses and churches from colonial times.

Yet, one does not feel quite at home in Bogotá. Something is wrong with the atmosphere—you have a feeling that you are in a city occupied by an enemy. People seem dejected and dissatisfied; it is obvious that they do not trust one another. When a storekeeper in the Colombian capital closes his shop for the night, he does not merely turn the key —he puts three to six solid padlocks on the door. Most people have no door mats, but if you do see one it is chained to the house. When people park their cars, they always take off the windshield wipers. If you pay anyone a silver coin, he will flick it with his nail and hold it up to his ear to make sure it is not counterfeit.

It must be hard for a boy scout to do his daily good turn in this atmosphere of mutual suspicion. On the main street of Bogotá I once saw a lady drop her bag. I hurried toward her, but as I bent down to pick it up, my gallant intentions were rewarded by a hard push—she thought I wanted to steal the bag!

It's quite understandable that the Bogotanians are so careful. The crime rate has been rising steadily ever since the big revolution that occurred a few months before our arrival. During the first twenty-four hours we spent in the capital, a total of 172 holdups and thefts were committed.

There is still a curfew in the capital. It is forbidden to be out of doors after midnight, and for those who are hard of hearing it is a risky business. You are not challenged by the police—they mutter, "Halt," as they cock their rifles, and if you do not obey instantly, a bullet will make certain that you do. Almost every night a couple of persons are shot by the overzealous enforcers of the law.

One of the most interesting places in Bogotá is a narrow street in the center of the town. I don't remember its name, but we called it "Babble Street." From morning till night it is black with people; you have to walk sideways and use your elbows to move through the crowd. There are any number of pickpockets and shoeshine boys; the latter kneel unperturbed in the throng, working busily with half-oranges which they use for cleaning their customers' shoes.

The people in "Babble Street" are mainly men. They talk incessantly. You have to speak loudly to make yourself heard, so everyone raises his voice—louder and louder they shout, yet they never succeed in drowning their neighbors' cries.

What do they talk about? The subjects men discuss everywhere in the world—women and politics. Judging by their talk, there must be an inexhaustible supply of virgins in Bogotá, because the girls seduced by these Don Juans are invariably innocent. If you listen to their political arguments, you will learn many expressive swearwords. You will also get a lot of hair and dandruff on your coat, because the men like to tear their black locks to illustrate how unjust and hopeless the world is.

And in a way they're right—life is tough in Colombia, both for rich and poor.

Two days after our arrival we got acquainted with a young engaged couple, both from wealthy families. One evening my wife suggested that we should all go to a movie. The girl hesitated.

"I'm not sure my parents would like it," she said. "They want one of my brothers to accompany me when I go out with Pedro."

We succeeded in convincing her that we were a respectable couple, quite capable of protecting her virtue. Chi-yun

74

then suggested a film with Charles Boyer. Once more the girl hesitated.

"There's a church at the next corner," she informed us. It seemed that this could have no possible connection with Charles Boyer, but it did. Just inside the church hung a long list of the movies being shown in town which had been censored by the archbishop. Love without the blessings of the Church, exposed legs, or low-cut dresses, prolonged kissing scenes—all these things were considered "improper." The Charles Boyer film was high on the list of the banned films, so we had to go to a comedy. It did not injure our souls, but to me it involved a good deal of spiritual torment —the plot was idiotic and the actors made so much noise that I couldn't even sleep.

Then we went to dine in an excellent French restaurant —if you want good food in Colombia, you must go to a place which has a foreign chef. As soon as we had finished eating, the girl wanted to return home.

"But we're going out to dance!" Chi-yun protested.

"Oh no—not without one of my brothers coming too!" said the girl. "My parents would be furious."

"Yes, I think we'd better take you home," Pedro put in. "I don't want your parents to worry about you." A thoughtful and well-brought-up young man, I said to myself. But as soon as we had delivered his betrothed to her anxious parents, he called up another girl and asked her to join the party. She was not nearly as chaste, and we realized that Pedro kept her as his mistress.

"I don't like being unfaithful to my girl friend," Pedro told me at one point during the evening. "But it's very difficult—I mean, we're never allowed to be alone."

75

Pedro was a nice lad and gave me a lot of good advice. "When you meet people here in Bogotá, always make it clear right away that you're not a North American," he said. "The Yankees aren't popular in Colombia."

That was putting it mildly. In a way I can understand why the Latins don't care for their big, northern neighbors. Generally speaking, Americans are just not suited to get along with sensitive natives. Formerly, the Germans had a strong influence in South America, and they got along fine with the local people—they learned Spanish, mixed with the Latins, and did everything possible to satisfy their customers. The South Americans could have all the credit they wanted, and the Germans exported goods especially made to suit their customers' demands.

The Americans are not like that. They make poor emigrants—if it is possible to call them emigrants at all, for they don't go to a foreign country to settle down, only to earn money and then return to the U.S.A. They usually do not learn the language; they have their own "sets" in all the big South American towns and keep to themselves as much as possible. Their business methods are tough—no credit, cash down, take it or leave it. The Latins had to take it during the war, because they could only obtain goods from the States.

But the hatred which many Colombians feel for Uncle Sam is, in my opinion, somewhat exaggerated. The Americans are blamed for almost everything except catastrophes of nature. Prices rise in Bogotá: the Wall Street speculators are pulling invisible wires. Coffee prices fall (the export of coffee is Colombia's main source of income): again the Shylocks of New York have been at work. First the North

Americans robbed Colombia of Panama; now they're trying to steal Colombia's oil, gold, and platinum.

Down on "Babble Street" I dared not raise my voice in defense of the Americans—lynching is not my idea of a pleasant form of death. But now, far away from Colombia, I have the courage to step forward and speak my mind.

It's true enough that Colombia's oil wells are run mainly by Americans. It is also true that the largest gold and platinum mines in the country are in American hands.

But why are they?

This is a question which the Colombian does not like to answer. Let us ask him some more. Why is only 3 per cent of all the land in the country under cultivation? Why do 95 per cent of the people live in poverty although there could and should be plenty for everyone? For there are less than seventy thousand who make more than $2,200 a year.

"Uh——ah——that's because . . . . ." Suddenly the Colombian smiles. "Oh yes!" he says, "that's because we lack communications, we have no roads or railways . . . . ."

Quite right. The lack of communications is a tremendous handicap. In Bogotá a cow costs more than 300 pesos ($153). In the mountains some 250 miles away you can buy a much bigger and fatter cow for 30 pesos ($15.30), but there are no roads, so you cannot send the animal to the capital. It is not only the Magdalena Valley which could be transformed into fertile meadows or fields. There is rich land everywhere, but it does not pay to cultivate it—you cannot get your products to the big markets.

But why are there no roads or railways?

Well, the Colombians say—it must be the fault of the government; the political situation . . . . .

77

To understand the political situation we must go back 120 years, to the time when Colombia tore itself away from Spain. I purposely avoid saying "the day Colombia gained its freedom." It was not a question of freedom for the people. More than anything else it was an economic question. At that time, Colombia was dominated by a few thousand rich Spanish families. They were tired of sending the largest part of their profits to Spain. Also, Madrid had offended them deeply by insisting that the overlords of the colony must be men born in Spain.

For nine-tenths of the population the revolution meant only that the reins changed hands. Now the rich families no longer owed allegiance to the Spanish crown. They put all the profits into their own pockets.

After the revolution, two political parties arose: Conservatives and Liberals. When the Conservatives were in power, the Church was given a free hand. When the Liberals got in, the government made lukewarm attempts to curb the influence of the priests. Otherwise, there was not much difference.

The people—mainly poverty-stricken peons of Spanish-Indian descent—received no education whatsoever. Once a year the peon went to the nearest town to vote. He understood only vaguely what it was all about; being unable to read or write, he merely put a cross against the name of the party to which his "patron" belonged.

It became a habit. Even today, you often meet Colombian workers or farmers with the reddest of red ideas who vote for the Conservatives—Father did, and he did it because Grandfather did, and he did it because his "patron" was a Conservative.

78

In the good old days, life must have been pleasant for the "patron." He was a little tin god: the poor doffed their hats and stepped into the gutter when he came strutting down the street. The people knew their place.

But as time passed, the proletarians began to think. Not many of them—only a few "saboteurs" who got their ideas from abroad. The existing social order was unjust, they claimed, and they wanted to change it. In the beginning these agitators were thrown into jail. The Church condemned them. However, it proved impossible to silence them, so it was decided to steal a march on them. The government passed a long series of impressive social laws, copied from Germany and the United States. Now the workers and the peons were suddenly to have free medical treatment, summer holidays with full pay, shorter working hours, and many other benefits.

It looked fine on paper; but, in reality, the poor were made to foot the bill. The city workers went on living in hovels and eating corn and beans. The peons are still worse off. A doctor who worked at one of the large estates told me about conditions in the country. The peons drink like fish, he said; uncleanliness is the cause of most of their sickness. A small scratch soon becomes an infected wound; eczema spreads all over the body. But the sick refuse to wash themselves, so the doctor could do nothing for them until he got a bright idea. He picked some harmless leaves, dried them, and gave them to the peons.

"Put these leaves in a big kettle of boiling water," he told them. "Wait until it cools off, and then rub yourselves thoroughly all over with the solution. The wounds will soon disappear."

79

The peons like to use medicine, so they obeyed. The wounds did disappear, and many a peon had his first bath since birth.

When the new social laws were passed, the cost of carrying them out was simply deducted from the pay of the workers and peons. "We have to do it," the employers explain. "Their working capacity has not increased—on the contrary, they drink more and work less than before, so of course we can't raise their wages."

The working capacity of the poor will not increase until they get better education and training; they will not receive this until they can afford to give their children a better upbringing and send them to school; they cannot afford to do so until they get higher wages. It sounds like a vicious circle.

The government does not seem to be trying very hard to get to the root of the evil. It is so easy to pass social laws; it's both dangerous and expensive to educate the people. And besides the government never has enough time. When the Liberals are elected, they immediately start tying the hands of the Church. When the Conservatives take over, they get busy undoing the knots. For many years the various governments were fully occupied with such important problems. Oil drilling, mining, and similar commercial undertakings were left to the North American materialists, who always had ready cash and paid well for concessions. Meanwhile, the owners of the big estates made good money, the factory wheels turned despite the lack of skilled labor, and life went on as usual.

But the poor became more restless, and in the spring of 1948 there was an explosion. The workers in the large cities became sick and tired of looking at the flashy American cars which the capitalists had imported instead of badly needed machinery for road-building and agricultural development. The living conditions of the peons had not improved despite golden promises—they had shorter working hours than before, but they got less to eat. A serious inflation was in progress.

Gaitán, a political leader with an agile tongue, became head of the radical section of the Liberal party. He flirted with the small but rapidly growing Communist party. On April 9 he was assassinated. It is still not known who instigated the murder. The Conservatives were in power at the time, but they disclaimed all responsibility. The workers accused the rich. Their idol had been killed, and they wanted revenge. An angry mob ran amuck in the capital. They stormed government buildings, captured the radio station, looted and burned hundreds of shops. Streetcars were torn off their tracks and destroyed. (Later the workers regretted this: they had to get up much earlier and walk to the factories.) The revolution spread to several other cities before it was finally crushed by government troops.

Bogotá's handsome face was badly marred. But soon the wounds began to heal. The burned houses were rebuilt; the shops were given new windowpanes. Slowly, almost unnoticeably, the government tightened its grip. Many progressive leaders were accused of being Communists and sent to jail. The Communist party was outlawed, but continued its work underground. The workers and peons went on chewing their beans; on "Babble Street" the people babbled more than ever, and of course the North Americans were blamed for Gaitán's murder.

Let us return to the Colombian whom we were questioning a little while ago—I hope he has not fallen asleep while listening. Shouldn't we ask him why there are practically no roads or railways, why Colombia is such a backward country despite its enormous possibilities? Colombia is a democratic nation. The government is elected by the people, so we must take it for granted that it represents the will of the people. Does that mean that the Colombians really lack sufficient energy and ability to run their own country properly? Does it mean that without North American initiative and capital the oil and the gold would be left underground?

In fact, that is precisely what it does mean. In an attempt to gain the support of the people by fanning nationalism, the government recently demanded a higher share of the profits made by foreign companies—too large a share, evidently, for most of the investors have decided to pull out of Colombia. Already most of the big oil fields and gold mines are practically deserted.

But the Colombian refuses to answer our questions. He is angry—I have attacked the honor of his country! It surprises him very much that I've been so tactless. After all, I am a European, and one doesn't expect such impertinence except from the vulgar, grabbing North Americans.

By Bus

to the Equator

I AM GLAD WE DID NOT MISS THE BUS RIDE FROM BOGOTÁ TO Quito—but I should hate to do it over again.

The road is a link in the famous Pan-American Highway which is going to be completed any day now—at least that is what the newspapers have been saying during the last few years, and they will probably still be saying it in 1971. The Canadians and the Americans have long since completed their parts of the highway, but there are still long stretches of the jungle in Central and South America where the surveyor hasn't set foot. Take it easy——haste makes waste——tomorrow is another day, say the Latins. Fortunately, for I dread the day when Coca Cola and other posters will form an unbroken wall from Rio Grande down to Cape Horn. Yet, I must admit that there were times on the trip when we longed for an ice-cold Coca Cola or a cushioned seat, but that was only in the beginning. Once you develop calluses on your behind it isn't so bad.

You soon learn to duck when you are in the bus. The moment you hear a gurgling sound from one of the other passengers, you had better lower your head in a hurry. I'm usually quite pleasant and easygoing, but I just cannot stand it when people vomit over me. The South Americans don't seem to mind such trifles. Neither do they get angry if a strong wind is blowing while a mother holds her baby out of the window—a slight sprinkling makes little difference when you're already filthy.

I once knew a lady who smeared her face with a muddy substance. It rejuvenated the skin, she said. If that were true, all the passengers on the bus would have gained the complexion of a newborn baby. From morning till night we drove in clouds of dust—we could hardly inhale a breath without filtering it through a handkerchief. The Equator wasn't far away, and dust plus sweat formed a dough which soon dried. Whenever we smiled, the beauty mask cracked. Then the perspiration broke out again, absorbed more dust, and the damage was repaired.

On the trip from Colombia to Ecuador one sees some of the most awe-inspiring views in the world. They take your breath away, partly because the road in many places has been blasted into almost perpendicular mountainsides from where you look straight down into yawning abysses. One moment the radiator points east, the next moment west, for the road zigzags endlessly as it winds its way up and down gigantic mountains. At nine in the morning you're on a plateau high up in the clouds: your teeth chatter despite overcoat and woolen underwear; the children whimper from cold; pigs run across the road, and they all have icicles hanging from their snouts, through which sticks have been stuck to prevent them from rooting up potatoes. At one o'clock in the afternoon you're down at sea level. The air vibrates with heat, and the mountains in the background seem liquid. You cannot very well take off your woolen underwear in the bus, so you just sit there half-unconscious, and feel your tongue swelling from heat and thirst.

The bus stops with a jerk—you open your eyes. What's that? Coal-black faces approach the window; white teeth sparkle in smiles that reach from ear to ear. An oasis, populated by Negroes. Their straw huts are built like African kraals. The people are naked except for colored kerchiefs tied round their hips. How they carry themselves, these Negroes! And what bodies they have: the firm breasts of the women are almost as big as the coconuts they hold up for sale! What a contrast their cheerful expressions are to the black, sullen faces in Panamá! Here the Negroes are happy. Why? Because they are allowed to be themselves, with no whites to look down on them or bully them.

When they came here many years ago, the valley was a desert. A river attempted to reach the sea, but evaporated before it got there. The Negroes dammed up the river and used its water to irrigate the dry earth which gave them rich reward for their labor. Nowhere in Colombia do you get finer tropical fruits at lower prices—juicy mangoes, fragrant pineapples the size of a man's head, bananas and sugar cane as thick as the wrist.

The driver filled the thirsty radiator, poured water on the hot decks, and off we roared into the desert while the Negroes waved good-by. Bone-dry clumps of sagebrush flew by as the bus climbed the steep foothills of the Andes; before long the oasis was only a green speck far below.

We yawned and swallowed to release the air pressure in our ears. The wind cut through our clothes and set the dust whirling over the barren hills. Sheltered behind rocks sat Indian shepherds who stared glassy-eyed at their scattered sheep; the animals had to run a mile or so to find a tuft of grass.

Mountain, valley; heat, cold; Negroes, Indians—so it went on for four days while we sat as if in a vise, six on each wooden bench, thirty people crammed together in an old Ford which had once been a truck. In the States, or in Europe, there would have been endless grumbles and complaints; but our fellow travelers were poor and simple people. They were used to walking, so they enjoyed the trip. Even when they were nearly choked with dust, they would laugh and joke.

"My province is as large as all the rest of Colombia," someone from this district would say.

"No, no," the others objected.

"Oh, yes," he insisted. "That is, if you flatten out all the mountains." And they would laugh until the tears came and made light streaks in the dark masks of mud.

In one of the towns where we stayed overnight, I happened to hear of a countryman of mine who had been arrested some weeks before. I went to the jail and was allowed to talk to him through a rusty iron grating. He looked tired and sick. Was there anything I could do for him? Sadly he shook his blond head. No, it was only a question of time. Everything took time in this part of the world; he had been there for many years and was used to it. I won't talk about his crime, because I only heard his side, but this is how one is treated in a Colombian jail.

After his arrest he was thrown into a cell with twenty-odd, hardened criminals. Five were murderers, the remainder holdup men and sexual perverts. As soon as the guard had shut the cell door, they knocked the new arrival out and robbed him of everything he possessed; he was only allowed to keep his pants, shirt, and shoes.

He dared not complain. If you blabbed to the guards, you risked being killed; two prisoners had been "liquidated" while he was in the jail. All he got to eat was bean soup, tortillas, and water. As soon as the lights were switched off at night, bedbugs swarmed out of their holes; it would have taken hours to count all his bites. If a prisoner did not behave, his wrists and ankles were chained together and he was put under solitary confinement in a pitch-dark cell where he could neither stand nor lie down.

In Colombia, he told me, you do not have to prove a man guilty. All you have to do is to sign an accusation against him—he's immediately put behind bars and will not be released until he can prove his innocence. One of the prisoners, a schoolteacher, had been accused of seducing a minor. The charges were proved false, so he was acquitted —but not released. The Columbian lawmakers lose all respect for a man who has been in jail. His reputation is ruined, and he will not be released until he can persuade three respected citizens to sign a bond for him. The poor schoolteacher was from another district; he had few friends in town, and nobody would stand bail for him. More than a month had passed since his acquittal, but he was still behind bars.

Later, I found out that the authorities in neighboring Ecuador are much more lenient. There a prisoner can get a private cell with an easy chair and a telephone—provided he can pay for it. If the food doesn't appeal to him, he can have meals sent from his home; and twice a week he is allowed to receive a lady visitor alone in his cell.

Before reaching Ecuador we had to submit to plain highway robbery. Early in the afternoon we arrived at the Colombian frontier town and went to the shed of the customs officer who was sitting at his desk, busy picking his teeth. Couldn't we see, he asked, that he wasn't working? It was Sunday, and Sunday was his day off, but . . . . .

I gave him a few pesos, and he chalked a mark on our suitcase without even opening it. The passport inspector was also sitting at his desk; it was his day off, too, but he also could be persuaded.

We hired an ancient taxi and drove to the International Bridge where an army of customs officers and passport inspectors were waiting for us. Before we could leave Colombia, our luggage must be checked, our passports stamped. It had just been done! Narrow shoulders shot up—so sorry, but it had to be done again here, and unfortunately it was Sunday, but for a small consideration . . . . .

It was the same story on the Ecuadorian side, only here were even more inspectors with outstretched hands. It was dark before we finally got through, so we went to a hotel, and at daybreak next morning we squeezed into a bus which was supposed to start at 4:00 A.M. with twenty-four passengers. It left at a quarter-past six with at least forty and did not reach Quito until late that night. I had always imagined that it was quite impossible to sleep while being jerked about in a bus, but now I know that it can be done, provided you are tired enough.

88

Bored

in Ecuador

IF YOU GLANCE CASUALLY AT THE MAP OF SOUTH AMERICA, you can easily overlook Ecuador which lies in the top corner to the left. It looks so tiny, squeezed in between the Pacific and its three mighty neighbors: Colombia, Brazil, and Peru. In size it is no larger than Texas, but it has almost as much variety to offer as all the rest of South America put together.

For Ecuador really consists of five different countries which have little in common except their flag, coinage, and capital. Five languages are spoken, and the population has five different colors: red, brown, black, yellow, and white.

Let us start with the most civilized part of the country —it is also the least interesting, so we can deal with it quickly. It can easily be traced on the map: like a writhing snake it follows the single-track railway which runs from north to south. At either end of the narrow strip lie the two largest cities in Ecuador—Guayaquil and Quito.

A few miles outside Quito you can stand astride the

Equator and at the same time almost touch the snowy caps of the surrounding mountain peaks: the city lies 9,300 feet above sea level. As soon as the sun goes down you had better put on your woolen underwear. It is a cozy place with a pleasant small-town atmosphere—only the main street tries to put on airs and appear sophisticated. Several of its buildings are four stories high, and at night, when the neon lights shine brightly, you can easily imagine yourself in a great modern metropolis.

But step inside the best grocery store in the capital—the one that advertises "guaranteed pasteurized milk." Ask for a bottle as we did, because I'm fond of milk. The owner of the store, a friendly German woman, leaned over the counter and whispered to me, "If you want to play safe, you'd better boil the milk."

And try to use the telephone—as we did on the first day. I wanted to talk to the Danish consul, but there was no phone at our hotel, so we went to a store. With pleasure, the manager said when I asked if we could borrow his phone; here was the directory . . . . .

It was the latest edition, ten years old. No Danish consulate was listed, so I called information. To the best of their knowledge, the Danish consul was a soap manufacturer. I asked for his number and after waiting five minutes, got the call. Danish consul? Soap manufacturer? No, this was a wineshop and had been one for the past eight years or more.

Again I called information. Sorry, the operator couldn't help me, but suggested that I call the other exchanges. There were five, and one of them might have heard of the Danish consulate.

The first exchange did not answer at all. The second was out of order. The third one had never heard of a country called *Dinamarca* and doubted if such a consulate existed. By now I was red in the face and began to raise my voice, but the manager put a restraining hand on my shoulder.

"If I were you, I'd forget it," he said. "Even if one has the right number, it's almost impossible to put a call through. We hardly ever use the phone—it's much quicker to send a messenger."

A few steps from the main street the asphalt is replaced by cobblestones, and low clay huts overhang the crooked alleys. If it is night-time you risk stumbling over a drunk, for the street lights are dim and the Ecuadorians consume a lot of *aguardiente.* After another few blocks the lamps and the cobblestones come to an end, and you walk on through mud or dust according to the season. Take a look at the churches on your way back to the hotel, and you've seen just about all there is to see in Quito.

Even the thought of Guayaquil, the largest city in the country, makes me perspire. It lies by the Pacific, an immense collection of wooden houses with corrugated-iron roofs. The most remarkable thing about the place is the Ecuadorian Navy, anchored in the muddy harbor. It consists of a former yacht with two guns mounted on deck, a torpedo boat, and a cruiser which the government bought from the United States at the end of the last war. When it was delivered, the Ecuadorians discovered that no crew could stay on board—the cruiser had been built for service in the North Atlantic, and under the sun of the Equator it became like an oven. But it does look impressive there in the harbor, and the people of Guayaquil are so very proud of it.

According to a local story, the two other ships of the Ecuadorian Navy were sent on a mission to the Galapagos Islands some years ago. They cruised about for nearly a month and then returned to the mother country with their mission unfulfilled. The Galapagos Islands, reported the admiral, were no longer there!

Guayaquil's population consists of Negroes, Spanish-Indian half-breeds, whites, and Chinese. Though only a small minority, the Chinese own all the good restaurants in the town and are prominent in its business world. So the government in Quito on one occasion decided that they ought to contribute a little toward the welfare of the rulers of the country. A special committee was appointed to study the status of the Chinese. It was unanimously agreed that they should be deported.

The frightened Chinese hurriedly sent a representative armed with 50,000 sucres ($3,700) to Quito, and as soon as the money had been distributed among the various members of the government, the committee unanimously agreed that the Chinese could remain after all.

But now the government had tasted blood, and the same performance was repeated every year. When inflation occurred, however, the amount which the Chinese had to pay was raised to 100,000 sucres ($7,400).

About ten years ago a Chinese consul came to Guayaquil. When it was nearly time for the annual tribute to be paid, his countrymen asked him to take the money to Quito. To their horror he refused, and went to the capital without a cent in his pocket. Next day he interviewed the government committee.

"I hear that you intend to deport the Chinese?" he said. Yes, that was true enough, was his answer.

"Very well," continued the consul. "We are ready to leave at a moment's notice. But we are poor people and, by international law, the Ecuadorian Government is obliged to pay for our passage. I have calculated how much it will cost— it will amount to between four and five million . . . . . "

Since then the Chinese in Guayaquil have had no more trouble.

One would expect the only two large cities in the country to be on friendly terms, but this is not so. Quito looks down on Guayaquil—which is quite natural, considering the situation of the capital; and people from the highlands are extremely unpopular down by the coast. Sometimes the mutual dislike breaks into open conflict, as it did once during our stay in Ecuador. The cause this time was a football game between a team from the highlands and one from Guayaquil. The game took place on neutral territory in a small town on a mountain slope about halfway between the two cities. This was a wise precaution, but it was not enough. The Guayaquil team scored the first goal, which infuriated the spectators from Quito to such an extent that they began hurling stones at the enemy players. Not to be outdone, the spectators from Guayaquil got busy stoning the Quito players. It soon developed into a free-for-all, with many wounded on both sides.

When news of the battle reached Quito, the government declared a state of seige. In Guayaquil, the authorities were not so quick. A mob soon gathered on the main street, clamoring for the blood of the enemy; and before the police could interfere, hundreds of windows had been broken in houses belonging to the "foreigners" from the highlands.

Most tourists see little of Ecuador beyond the two large cities. They arrive in Quito on the morning plane, take a quick glance at the Equator Monument and the churches, and fly on to Guayaquil in the afternoon. Here they drink a couple of whiskies at the hotel, then hurry away to the relative coolness of Lima, convinced that Ecuador is a thoroughly uninteresting country.

Chi-yun and I could easily have done likewise, but fortunately we made friends with a European who had lived for many years in Quito. He shook his head disapprovingly when he heard that we wanted to go to Peru.

"But you've only been here a few days," he said.

"Anyway we're bored," I replied. "There's nothing for me to write about in this country."

"Young man, you don't know what you're talking about. I've read practically all the books on Ecuador. Twice as many could be written, and there would still be lots of material for you hungry writers. Of course, you won't learn a thing by sitting here in Quito. You must go out into the country. Why don't you go down to Esmeraldas—that's on the Pacific coast, a Negro settlement populated by descendants of African slaves who ran away from their masters and hid in the jungle. It isn't easy to get there— you have to go by truck to the foot of the Andes and then continue by canoe. But it's worth the trouble, if only to hear their drums at night and see them dance round their fires. They live the life of Riley—lie under the trees and wait for the fruits to ripen.

"If that's too far for you, go to Santo Domingo de los Colorados—that's about halfway between here and Esmeraldas. You've heard about the Colorado Indians, haven't you? They're the most interesting tribe in all South America, I think—just wait until you get there.

"There's lots to be written about the Indians in the highlands, too, and about those in the Oriente—that's what we call the lowlands east of the Andes; it's really a part of the Amazon Valley. One of the tribes down there is called the Aucas. They're stark naked, but you won't ever see them— they kill all foreigners. Eat them afterward. Unpleasant people altogether, and not too well liked by their neighbors, the Jibaro Indians. They're the head-hunters . . . . ."

"Head-hunters?" I interrupted. "In Colombia, I heard about a Danish couple who've settled down among the head-hunters somewhere in Ecuador. I wanted to pay them a visit, but no one seemed to know where they are. As far as I remember, their name is Holtved . . . . ."

"I know them," he said. "Met them before they went into the jungle nearly a year ago. I don't think anyone has heard from them since."

"Do you suppose we could find them?"

"I don't see why not—I know approximately where they are—but you must go west first. Let me draw a rough map for you—look, here's Quito in the middle. You go down this way, to the Colorados. The trip won't take more than two days. Then you return to Quito and go south. Stop on the way and visit the Arends brothers—they have a truck farm near Ambato and can tell you all about the highland Indians. From there, it's only a day's journey down to the jungle where the Holtveds live . . . . ."

Not Barbarians, Please

FROM QUITO THE ROAD WENT DOWN, DOWN UNTIL OUR eardrums seemed about to burst. The dry, cold mountain air disappeared behind us and we drove into steaming jungle. When the sun was about to set, the truck stopped with screeching brakes in a broad village square. We were in Santo Domingo, the capital of the Colorado Indians.

But no Indians live in Santo Domingo itself. The population consists of mestizos who trade with the jungle people. Around the square lie some fifty wooden huts built on stilts. Two of them—the church and the Grand Hotel—are much taller than the others. The hotel is the finest building in the village. There's a bar and a restaurant on the ground floor, and behind them stands a rusty iron drum. The people of Santo Domingo often glare at it as they walk by—what's the sense of having a toilet, when the jungle is only a few feet away? But the hotel manager insists on keeping it—for the convenience of the foreign visitors, he explains.

96

He personally guided us to our room on the second floor and promised to procure mules for the next day's trip into the jungle. As soon as we entered, I pointed out that the sheets on the two narrow metal beds looked none too clean. Our host couldn't understand it. The sheets had been changed last Saturday, he said; at the Grand Hotel, the sheets were always changed once a week. If we wanted to wash ourselves, we would find a washbasin in the corridor, but please use the water sparingly, as it was carried here from a river in the jungle. He also requested us not to throw our slops out of the window into the street, as it annoyed those who were hit by them.

When he left, we took off most of our clothes and lay down on the beds. Our shoes we kept on; if you put a bare foot on the floor, the sole immediately became black. The little room seemed to have absorbed all the heat of the day through the corrugated-iron roof. Slowly the long shadows of evening slid by the open window; in the semi-darkness, the huts looked like giants on stilts. The cicadas raised their voices to a raucous chorus. Twice we heard faint splashing. Our neighbors considered the climb down to the iron drum a waste of time; it was much easier to use the window.

At seven o'clock it was pitch-dark. The trip had tired us, and we were about to fall asleep when an engine was suddenly started—the local power plant. It coughed twice, and then there was light. We heard many other noises and went to the window to see what was happening.

From all the huts, people came down steps and ladders. Within a few minutes several-dozen tents and portable booths had been set up beneath flickering electric-light bulbs strung over the market square. Now we understood why there were only two small shops in Santo Domingo. Nobody wanted just to go in, put his money on the counter, and say: I want so and so. It was much more fun to buy a lottery ticket, throw dice, or play roulette; and you could win almost anything that way, if you were lucky—knives, needles, American cigarettes, buttons, canned food, a pound of white sugar, envelopes, sunglasses, soap. Usually, though, the gamblers won only a button or a needle.

In the bar down below glasses of *aguardiente* were emptied as quickly as the bartender could fill them. Before long the voices became loud and quarrelsome. About eight o'clock devilish noises came from the movie theater which had opened its door. It was an American gangster film; the spectators shouted with joy as the guns blazed. In a dance hall nearby, people jitterbugged and *rumba'd* violently despite the heat. Most of the girls were barefoot, but two or three of them wore high-heeled shoes and had much powder and lipstick on their faces. Every once in a while, one of them would disappear into the jungle with a man. On these expeditions, the girls always carried their shoes in their hands.

Only a few people seemed to notice the tall figures which approached silently from the jungle. For a while they stood in the shadow of a hut, watching the lively spectacle. Then they took courage and stepped into the lighted square.

When you see a Colorado Indian for the first time, you feel like exclaiming, as the country yokel did on seeing a giraffe, there ain't no such animal! Even if you met him at a carnival, you'd hardly believe your own eyes. He is tall, well built, and his entire body has been painted with a strong, red color. That thing on his head—is it a red base-ball cap? No, it's his own hair, plastered with clay and plant juices. The stiff bangs come almost to the nose while the neck is clean shaven. When the clay hardens, the Indian has an excellent headgear. True, it can't be doffed, but it protects against sun and rain, and it's decorative.

His naked torso and muscular arms are painted with dark, horizontal stripes. Narrower stripes ornament his face, and on his wrists are broad, silver bracelets. Around the hips he wears a short, red-cotton cloth. From the knees down, the legs are dyed coal black.

The man is invariably followed by his squaw, whose full, naked breasts rise and fall with every step. A blue circle has been drawn round each nipple, but her body is not painted red. Around her neck hang half-a-dozen strings of colored beads, half-covered by her loose black hair which reaches to the shoulders. Her only piece of clothing is a dark-red skirt.

From our window we watched the Indians walking from booth to booth. There were eight or nine of them, and they looked like proud kings among the noisy, gesticulating city dwellers. Their faces were as expressionless as masks, but nothing seemed to escape their attention.

They stopped before the biggest roulette wheel. "Try your luck for a sucre!" cried the croupier with a quick glance toward them. "For only one sucre you can win a cooking pot, a bottle of firewater—even a box of colors for painting yourselves!"

The bystanders burst out laughing, and we could see the tallest Indian's mouth twitch slightly. It was difficult to tell whether he was amused or annoyed—perhaps he did not even understand Spanish. The little group now walked toward the movie theater and looked in through the half-open door. Judging by the noise, a decisive battle was taking place between gangsters and G-men. The spectators shouted with excitement. But after a few minutes the Indians walked away.

A girl came toward them, a girl with high-heeled shoes. I suppose she had had too much to drink; otherwise she probably wouldn't have tried to attract an Indian. Or maybe she did it only for fun. We could not hear what she said, but it was easy to imagine, for she put her hand on his arm and smiled enticingly.

The Indian just looked at her. Her eyes wavered, the smile disappeared, her face hardened. ". . . . . Indian!" she shouted as she let go of his arm and hurried toward the bar.

Unperturbed, the jungle people continued on their stroll. When half an hour or so had passed, they walked back into the forest. They had bought nothing. Why had they come at all?

Why do we go to the zoo?

*   *   *

It was the first time Chi-yun had gone into the jungle, and she did not like it. Mosquitoes buzzed about us in the dark tunnels which wound their way through the forest; the horses slipped in the ankle-deep mud; branches with prickly leaves whipped our faces. Hot vapors rose from the ground where ticks and leeches lay waiting to burrow into the flesh of innocent travelers.

After three hours we reached a river that had dug a deep chasm through the jungle. Here we had to dismount and continue on foot. Our guide, an unshaven mestizo, told us that we would soon come to a large Colorado Indian farm.

So we did, but no one was to be seen when we got there. The house lay in a clearing on top of a hill and was almost as large as the Grand Hotel. The roof was of straw, its ridge covered by a split and hollowed-out tree trunk, about forty feet long, which protected it against wind and weather.

"Buenos tardes," shouted our guide. There was no answer, so we walked to the entrance. A hen clucked, calling her chickens together, and nervously led them inside. There were no windows, but the rough wallboards were nailed together in such a way that there was an inch gap between them, letting in the light in narrow, slanting streaks. This made the house cool and enabled the inhabitants to watch anyone who approached.

In one corner inside a woman was busy weaving. She must have been in her late forties, but her skin was smooth and surprisingly light in color. When we entered, she answered the guide's greeting with a curt nod and immediately rose and led us outside again; I suppose she didn't like having strangers in the house. Out of a corner of her eye she saw me winding my camera. Quickly, she raised her arms to cover her bosom.

All the other people of the house had gone to the market in Santo Domingo, she told us in hesitant Spanish. They would not return until sundown.

She stood still, waiting for us to go. "Won't you let me take a picture of you?" I asked. She shook her head; the Colorado Indians don't waste words. "Of course I'm willing to pay you," I added, holding out a five-sucre note. Five sucres is a lot of money in Ecuador—although in U.S. money a sucre is worth only seven cents—but she returned to the house without even answering or deigning to look at us once more.

"Impossible, these Indians!" said our guide with a hungry glance at the money. "Even one hundred sucres can't make them do anything if they don't want to. They could get big money out of the tourists, but they only shake their stupid heads. But never mind—in Quito you can buy plenty of post cards of them."

At the foot of the hill lay a large, neat pigsty. The pigs were almost black—they usually are in these parts—and had long, stiff bristles. The guide told us that the Colorado Indians supply Santo Domingo and the entire surrounding district with pork, though they seldom eat it themselves. Their diet consists mainly of corn and vegetables.

We could not persuade our guide to tell us much more about the Indians. Although he had always lived in Santo Domingo, he knew little about them, and he was not interested. But he promised to lead us to a famous Colorado witch doctor, and on our way there we had a stroke of luck —a blond, hollow-cheeked young man suddenly appeared on the path before us. Behind him walked a mule with a gasoline drum tied to its back, and astride the drum sat a small, yellow-haired boy.

"Hello!" the young man greeted us in broad American and for the next twenty minutes we listened to him, so absorbed that we hardly noticed the furious assaults of the mosquitoes. He was a Protestant missionary and had spent two years among the Colorado Indians.

"Yes, they seem unfriendly," he said. "But remember that they've been pestered by tourists—excuse my being so frank. And they've been gypped by all the traders in Santo

Domingo, so they don't think very highly of white people. But once you get to know them they're really quite nice."

Had he succeeded in converting any of them?

"Not one—it takes time. Officially they're Catholics, but they really worship their old gods—at least that's my impression, although I can't get them to talk about their religion. They never discuss that sort of thing with strangers. Their moral laws are very strict. Theft and dishonesty are almost unknown among them. They aren't wedded by the church, but I've never heard of one of the men being unfaithful to his wife."

There were only between six and seven hundred Colorado Indians, he told us—"as far as I know, the tribe has never been very large. Nobody knows where they came from or how long they've been here; their language has nothing in common with the other South American language groups. They never leave the tribe or marry outsiders, and under no circumstances will they work for a white or a mestizo. My wife and I have to get along without a servant—you see, we live in the jungle, and the Santo Domingo people refuse to come out to our place. Every Indian raises his own corn and vegetables and keeps pigs—they're great hunters and sell the pigs to get money for guns and ammunition. And for buying perfume, I mustn't forget that. The women are crazy about scent. They practically bathe in it, and when there's a feast you can smell them twenty feet away. That's an innocent enough pleasure, but unfortunately they also smoke and drink an awful lot. They start when they're four or five—yes, even the children drink liquor and smoke cigars —and twice a week the whole family gets dead drunk."

When we parted, he told me not to write anything that

would make "his" Indians seem like barbarians. "Maybe I oughtn't to say it," he added, "but in many respects they're better people than a lot of Christians."

We wished him good luck and continued on our journey. About half an hour later we came to the witch doctor's hospital, a large, open shed with some fifteen people inside it. Not one of them was an Indian. Some had made primitive beds out of boards and branches; others lay on the ground. Only those who were well off had blankets and mosquito nets. What ailed them I don't know, but several of them looked as if they had not long to live.

A stout, elderly woman, who was not a patient, offered us a cup of coffee. She had arrived a few hours before with her sick daughter. They had not even seen the witch doctor yet; he was out in the forest gathering herbs and probably would not return until the next morning.

"He's our last hope," the woman said. "My daughter has been examined by all the specialists in Guayaquil and Quito. Their bills came to many thousand sucres, but neither their treatments nor their medicines did her any good. It's a strange sickness. She gains weight all the time—now she weighs more than two hundred pounds although she's only eighteen, and her pulse becomes weaker. During the last two months she hasn't even been able to walk, and it was terribly difficult to have her carried here through the jungle."

She raised the mosquito net under which her daughter lay. We saw a white face and a pair of dark, uncomprehending eyes. On the bed next to her lay a Peruvian, yellow-skinned and thin as a skeleton. The doctors in his own country had also given him up.

We drank the coffee and returned to Santo Domingo.

Nearly a month later, when we were on our way down to Guayaquil, we met the stout woman on the train. Next to her sat her daughter, smiling and healthy!

"Yes, the Colorado doctor saved her," said the mother with a proud glance at the young girl. "It is difficult to recognize her, isn't it? She has already lost forty pounds, and she's still losing. The Peruvian was cured, too. Oh, he's a genius, that old witch doctor!"

How had he treated the young girl?

"I hardly know," answered the mother. "He didn't give her anything but herbs and water, and then he talked a lot with her; or he would just sit and hold her hand. She isn't allowed to eat meat, but otherwise she can have almost anything she likes."

"And how much did he charge you?"

"Three sucres."

Cabbage Kings

I OFTEN THINK OF THE TWO DANES BENDING OVER THEIR carrots and cabbages down on the other side of the Equator. In a way I pity them; but at the same time I envy them, for Kai and Paul Arends have found what most of us are still searching for. Let me try to express myself in a way which the brothers would understand. They love plants, and they have almost become plants themselves—two big carrots, rough on the surface and with most of the tops blown away by the wind. It wouldn't much surprise me if one of these days they took root in their own vegetable beds.

Farmers often come to feel at one with the soil. The strange thing about the Arends brothers is that they're really city people—or were. Both of them graduated from the University of Copenhagen before they left Denmark. Kai Arends went to Guayaquil in Ecuador where he became manager of a large Danish pharmacy. He made good money and lived well. As the years passed, his paunch increased—

you drink too many whiskey and sodas when in the tropics.

Paul got a job with a telegraph company which sent him to Siberia. He went through the Russian revolution and was later transferred to Finland. Here it was that he surprised his boss by suddenly sending in his resignation.

"But I thought you liked your work," said the boss.

"I do," Paul answered, "but there isn't enough of it—one hour in the morning, one in the afternoon, and that's all. I want some work that occupies all my time—not dead machines, but living plants."

In 1940 the brothers began writing to each other. Kai was tired of standing behind the counter all day and going to parties at night; besides, his liver and kidneys had started to complain at the inconsiderate treatment. Paul was running a small truck farm outside Helsinki, but his fear and dislike of the Communists made him want to get far away. Early in 1941 he went to Ecuador, where he and his brother bought Zamanga. I have forgotten to mention that in the meanwhile they had acquired wives and children—somehow, other questions always seem to come first at Zamanga. Instead of asking after their families you say: How are the potatoes doing? Will the peas soon be ready?

When the brothers took over the place, it had little to recommend it except the location. When you stand in the center of the farm, you can, if the day is clear, distinguish four or five volcanoes in the background. The mountains slope gently down to a green valley; the air is always dry and fresh. The temperature can suddenly fall from eighty to forty degrees, but it is never too hot or too cold. One finds it hard to believe that Zamanga lies only three steps in seven-league boots from the Equator.

Kai and Paul paid 15,000 sucres—then about $2,000 in American money—for eighty acres. It was a high price, for the soil yielded less than $100 annually.

When you shake hands with the brothers, you realize how hard they have worked. The calluses are thick and hard as stone. Their fingers have become stiff and unmanageable; above the wrists, bunches of muscles jut out. Kai's paunch has long since worn away.

They built their own home, a low farmhouse with many rooms and no fancy business. Every morning they rose at five and did not stop working until it became too dark to distinguish useful plants from weeds. The earth was plowed and fertilized, irrigation ditches were dug, fruit trees planted.

In South America only the poor work in the real sense of the word. Better-class people use only their heads, and sparingly at that. Those who earn their bread by the sweat of the brow are looked down on.

The two brothers were looked down on. They had two day laborers, but soon discovered that if they wanted anything done properly they had to do it themselves. The highland Indians were best at idling.

People laughed at the brothers. "In Quito or Guayaquil you can invest your money in shares that'll give you an annual return of 25 per cent," they said, and that was true enough—rich Ecuadorians consider it poor business if they make less than 20 per cent annually on their investments. "And instead of doing that," people continued, "you buy a piece of land and try to compete with the Indians. It just can't be done—remember that they can live on ten cents a day, they can sell their produce for less than a fifth of what you'll have to charge. You'll be ruined."

Paul and Kai said nothing. It has never been necessary for them to boast of what they've done. Facts speak for themselves. Today Zamanga is the finest truck farm in Ecuador. The brothers have a comfortable income and could sell the place for many times what they paid for it. But they still rise at five every morning, and even after the Saturday bath there are half-moons of dirt under their broken fingernails. If they did stop working, the diplomats and foreign business people in Quito and Guayaquil would not know what to do. Who else could supply them with the huge baskets of fruit and vegetables which they receive once a week from Zamanga? It would be necessary to have them flown in from the States, for no Ecuadorian can grow such fine produce.

Kai and Paul could earn big money. They could double their prices, and the foreigners would still be glad to pay. They could specialize in certain medicinal plants which, they know, are much more profitable than carrots and radishes. But they don't care a hang about money. They like to raise all the plants which can grow on the highland and are useful. They are always experimenting. If they discover that a certain Japanese herb thrives well at Zamanga, they'll say, "Very interesting." Maybe they will sell it at fifteen cents a pound, but the next day they will sow turnips which will bring them a cent a pound—if the price does not fall meanwhile.

What's the use of money to them, anyway? They have not bought any new clothes since they arrived at Zamanga, and they have not worn socks more than twice since then. Their toes stick out of their dirty sneakers; their shirts are patched and there are holes in their dungarees. It provides ventilation, the brothers say with a smile in their pale-blue eyes. The nearest town is ten miles away, and it does not tempt them in the least; if Lana Turner came to fetch them in a shiny Cadillac, she would have a hard time persuading them to go to the movies with her.

My wife and I spent ten days at Zamanga. One evening after dinner I made a little speech about Confucius, just to be entertaining. Kai Arends glanced at the clock. I attempted to start a discussion about modern American literature. Paul Arends yawned. Then I began talking about soybean production in China, and at once the two brothers came to life—they had thought of raising soybeans and wanted some information. In two minutes it was clear they knew much more about the subject than I did.

They are educated people who speak four languages and have read the classics; but what we consider an intellectual tidbit doesn't appeal to their palates at all. They have picked and chosen, and have come to the conclusion that life itself—a sprouting seed, the growth of a plant—is far more exciting than all the books in the world.

Bridge is their only real interest besides agriculture. Paul Arends' long, horselike face lights up with a smile at the mention of the word. Kai rubs his red, swollen hands and takes out the cards. Every night we played until the small hours, and they won five dollars from us although we held the better cards.

But when it was the night for watering, the game stopped early. Zamanga's thirst is quenched by a large canal from the mountains; every seventh day it is put at the disposal of the brothers who then have to go out with flashlights and make sure that all the beds get ample to drink. About ten o'clock their interest in bridge suddenly lessened regardless of whether a grand slam had been bid, doubled, and redoubled; and when they heard the water beginning to gurgle in the ditches they jumped up and went out.

One wonders why they have not been infected by Ecuador's most common disease, laziness. They do not look down on the indolent natives—they think of them as a kind of plant which does not grow very tall, and are amused by them. Thanks to the two brothers, I gained at least a superficial knowledge of the highland people.

Nature has supplied Ecuador with almost everything that man can desire. The soil is rich, there is oil, no lack of minerals or waterpower. Only one thing is missing—dissatisfaction. That may sound strange, but if people are to work hard they must have something to work for, some aim—you must hold a carrot in front of their noses. In the civilized countries we have many carrots. Daily, we are exposed to fresh temptations—when we have acquired a radio, we want a refrigerator; and as soon as we have bought one, we start saving up for a car. We earn more, buy more, yet we never can get enough.

The Ecuadorian has nothing, and yet he has enough. There's nothing he wants—no, perhaps that is not quite true. There are certain things he would like to have—but not if acquiring them means extra work. He is content to drink lukewarm water rather than to earn enough money by hard work to buy an icebox.

Nobody needs to starve in Ecuador, and very few do. The poorest people in the country are the day laborers on the highland—for instance, those who work at Zamanga. Most of them own a small piece of land. They have seen how the two Danes have trebled the productivity of the soil by taking proper care of it and by using fertilizers. But do the day laborers go home and do likewise? No—their forefathers did not do it. It requires initiative and capital, and besides it is much easier not to do it.

Their wages are about eighteen cents a day, which is enough to feed a whole family. They eat corn bread, beans, vegetables, and occasionally a little meat. Shoes they never wear, and their dress consists of a shirt, trousers, and a thick, dark-red woolen poncho which lasts a whole life-time and becomes warmer with the years, since it is never washed. It protects them against rain and wind and makes an excellent cover for the night. The highland Indians have no use for beds; they just lie down on the earthen floor and pull the ponchos around them.

Once the Arends had some important work which had to be done the next day, a Sunday. They asked the day laborers whether any of them would be willing to come then for double pay. Nothing doing! Sunday was their day of rest; and even if they got three times their usual pay they wouldn't work. But Kai Arends knows his Indians. "Will you work tomorrow if I give you as much *aguardiente* as you can drink?" he asked. The men clapped their hands. *Aguardiente!* Of course they would work!

There were six laborers, and they worked all that Sunday. At five in the afternoon Kai brought them a big pail of firewater. They lost consciousness before they could drink it all, and it had cost him less than one-fourth of what he would have had to pay them in wages.

When the highland Indian can get away with it, he will stay at home and do nothing while his wife works. The Arends have an Indian laborer who is fairly reliable but has one bad habit—he gets drunk every Sunday and never shows up for work on Monday morning. And every Saturday he invents a new excuse for his coming absence: his mother is to be buried, his son is sick, or something like that.

One Saturday he came with a brand-new excuse—he and his wife had to go to town to buy seed potatoes for their own fields. Of course the Arends could not object to that, but the following Saturday he said the same thing.

"Listen, you'll have to think up something better than that!" joked Kai. "After all, you said that last week."

"But it's really true!" the Indian assured him. "Last Monday we went to town and bought 160 pounds of potatoes. My wife can't carry more than 80 pounds at a time, so this coming Monday we must go to town, so she can carry the rest home."

The Indians have no stables for their domestic animals: the pig, the cow, and the chickens sleep under the same roof as the rest of the family. Maybe the air becomes rather thick in the dark, little room, but the nights are cold on the highland and the animals help to keep the place warm. If the owner of the house built a stable, he would also have to get a stove, and a stove eats firewood—no, as soon as you try to raise your standard of life, it becomes a vicious circle. Better be satisfied with what you have, says the Indian; after all, the good God gave us only one life, and it's up to us to get as much as possible out of it. Why be like the senseless foreigners who have time for nothing but work?

And so says the Negro who lies in the shade of the palm tree down by the coast, waiting for the fruits to ripen; so says the head-hunter in the jungle valley, the source of the Amazon, the Mother of Rivers.

A Walk
in the Jungle

THE RIDE DOWN TO THE ORIENTE TAKES A WHOLE DAY. You leave the highland early in the morning and about five hours later arrive at Baños, which is halfway. Here the air becomes damp and oppressive, and the brown mountains are hidden beneath luxuriant vegetation.

Baños means "baths." Boiling-hot sulphur water comes oozing out of countless cracks in the rocks, and travelers always stop and bathe in one of the many pools in the town. It is a tradition. They do it partly because the water is said to have healing powers, partly because they want to ensure good luck for the rest of the trip.

For Baños is a holy town. Its patron saint is Our Lady of the Holy Water, who undoubtedly would be offended if one omitted to take a dip. During the last hundred years she has performed so many miracles at Baños that even skeptics cannot explain them away as mere coincidences. And when she has saved her children, she always makes a personal appearance, floating on a little white cloud. The whole population has seen her, time and again.

On the plaza lies the cathedral, a building which is many times larger than it ought to be for so small a town. It is more impressive than beautiful. The great inner walls are decorated by some sixty murals which illustrate all the Lady's local miracles.

The Lady's worst enemy is Tungurahua, whose white helmet rises toward the sky more than 5,000 feet above Baños. Tungurahua is one of the largest active volcanoes in the world; beneath its innocent-looking crown of snow smolder the fires of hell. Periodically, hot steam will suddenly shoot from its head, and then both the mountains and Baños begin to tremble. The snow melts, and the steam is followed by glowing lava which usually flows through the same deep channels down toward Baños. Closer and closer comes the seething mass—the wooden buildings of Baños carbonize in the heat, the hair and clothes of the desperate people burst into flame as they kneel before the statue of the Holy Lady, which has been carried outside the cathedral so that she can see with her own eyes how great is the danger. The Holy Lady must have a strong sense of the dramatic, because she always waits until the very last moment before she comes down from the heavens on her little cloud. And immediately—the stream of lava stops, the mountains cease to tremble, and soon afterward a new mural will be painted in the cathedral to commemorate yet another miracle.

About five miles to the east of Baños lies a waterfall which is much higher than Niagara. A muddy column of water, thick as a house, spurts out of a mountainside and roars down into a chasm so deep that even a brave man feels faint when he looks into it. Until a few years ago there was only one tree trunk in the district which was long enough and strong enough to span the abyss. Travelers would shut their eyes tightly, make the sign of the cross, and pray fervently as their mules slowly crossed over that rough bridge. Sometimes the animal would stumble—beast and burden hurled to certain death? Not always! More than once the Holy Lady has come floating down at that moment—the animal falls and is crushed against the rocks far below, but the man with an immortal soul grabs hold of a bush which has suddenly appeared on the perpendicular mountainside. With a last effort he pulls himself up onto a ledge which also has never been there before . . . . .

The murals are not works of art. In most of them Tungurahua resembles an ice-cream cone or an exploding cigar, and the figures clinging to the sides of the abyss are more like monkeys than human beings. Yet, when you look at these amateurish paintings, your brow is liable to become wet with perspiration—in the solemn stillness of the church the incredible seems credible, and you yourself are shortly going to cross the chasm beneath the pale face of Tungurahua.

Fortunately the Shell Company has come to the aid of the Holy Lady, by taking over her arduous job as guardian angel of the abyss. The Ecuadorians would doubtless have continued indefinitely to rely on her powers, but about eight years ago the foreign oilmen decided that this practice couldn't go on forever. A solid-steel bridge was constructed, a road was made—the company had begun to sniff for oil deep inside the Ecuadorian jungle and needed what they considered more reliable communications.

They are still sniffing. Millions of dollars have been sunk in the experiment, and wells have been drilled to a depth of more than a mile; but so far the jungle has yielded only malaria and poisoned arrows. The work is carried on in strict secrecy, but rumors have leaked out that more than a dozen of the company's employees have been killed by the Aucas Indians, who are cannibals.

We stopped in the middle of the bridge, got out of the truck, and looked down. Even the thought of it still gives me an unpleasant feeling in the stomach. The driver threw a stone down, and seconds passed before we could see the white splash where it had hit the water.

Then we drove on, along the foaming river. Up here it was young and beautiful; joyfully it hurled itself against rocks and carved great hollows out of the mountains. But later on, when it had used up its strength, it ran tamed and exhausted through the flat Brazilian jungle.

We could see it grow whenever we came to a tributary. There was the White River, clear as glass; you almost felt sad to see it disappear into the muddy main stream. There was the Red River which had the color of coagulated blood. And at the Yellow River, the driver, of course, had to make the obvious remark about its lemon hue.

The forest grew denser, the trees taller in their struggle to reach the light. The sun was visible only as a flickering spot above the jungle haze. Every few miles we would pass laborers armed with shovels and pickaxes, who were striving to prevent the jungle from reconquering the road.

About four o'clock we arrived at Shell-Mera, from where

the oil company flies supplies to its drilling camps in the jungle. It is possible to reach these camps on foot, but it takes from three to four days and is not without danger. The airplane makes the trip in fifteen minutes.

Some distance beyond Shell-Mera the road stopped, and we were in Puyo, the entrance to what the writers of travel books call "The Green Hell" or "The Green Paradise"—it all depends on whether they have been there or whether they've been sitting in an easy chair, dreaming their way through the jungle. The latter alternative is more advantageous—you save the travel expenses, probably also a doctor's bill afterward, and the great reading public prefers romanticism to realism.

Puyo consists of close to a hundred huts; only one of them has a corrugated-iron roof, and here lives the commandant. We went to see him immediately on our arrival, and were received by a small man with a neat mustache and a big gun dangling from his belt. His was the task of ruling a jungle area about the size of Maine. On the ground outside the door sat his army, twenty-odd, barefoot soldiers who were busy rolling cigarettes.

We told the commandant everything we knew about the people we were looking for. It was not much. In Bogotá we had met an engineer who told us that his brother, Aage Holtved, lived with his wife in the Ecuadorian jungle. He gave me the impression that the couple were a bit odd. Not exactly crazy, but—hum, you know—they never wrote letters, and it did seem strange to settle down among the head-hunters. In Quito we had further learned that the Danes lived somewhere in the Puyo area, that they were tall and blond. All this I told the commandant.

118

He shook his head—first, he had never heard of the two Danes; secondly, under no circumstances would he permit us to go into the jungle to find them. The head-hunters did not like visitors, and his past experiences with gringo tourists had been unpleasant. Some years ago four American visitors had used a five-hundred-sucre note to tempt two natives to commit murder. An innocent mestizo had been killed, and afterward the Americans had taken moving pictures of what they believed was the famous head-shrinking process. In fact, the head had never become any smaller, and the whole thing had been reported to Quito to the commandant's great inconvenience.

Most deplorable, we admitted—but that was the sort of thing you could expect from gringos, wasn't it? With us it was quite different, of course—we were not Americans, nor were we in the least interested in shrunken heads.

I can't do it, but Chi-yun knows how to pour on the charm. Five minutes after she had flashed her first smile at the commandant, she could have wrapped him around her little finger. He called up one of his soldiers—Roberto, he said, was one of the best guides in the Oriente. Perhaps he could help us to find our blond couple; in any case, he put Roberto at our disposal and wished us good luck for the journey.

We went out on the road with Roberto, a muscular mestizo with thin lips and skeptical brown eyes. He had heard of a foreign couple who lived some distance away, but wasn't sure if they were the right ones. How long would it take to reach their place? Maybe one day, maybe three or four—who knows? Could he get any mules for us?

Mules? He looked at me as if I weren't quite right in

the head. No mule could go through the jungle. If we wanted to make the journey, we'd have to walk.

All right, we would walk. Yes, he said, but the question was whether we *could*. It would be a hard trip.

"My wife is much tougher than she looks," I remarked.

"It isn't so much the *señora* I'm worried about," he said. Then it could only be me. I hate reference to my rather slight build and informed him bitingly that I was no weakling. I had been in the jungle many times before, in distant lands which he hadn't even heard of——

"We'll see," he interrupted. "I want twenty sucres a day for being your guide, and you must bring along food for five days—hard-boiled eggs, bread, and cheese are most suitable. We will leave at five in the morning."

To our surpise he arrived on the stroke of five. We could hardly see him as we stepped out onto the road; it was still dark and a drizzling rain was falling. Without even a good morning, he suggested that we postpone the trip.

"But why?" I asked.

"The paths are almost impassable when it rains."

"A little water can't make all that difference," I replied.

"As you wish. But take off your coats and let me carry them. And haven't you got any better footwear?"

Who did the fellow think he was? I wore a pair of walking shoes; Chi-yun had on short boots that came just above the ankles. Our coats protected us against the rain and the raw morning cold. Roberto, on the other hand, looked quite laughable in white shorts, a polo shirt, and a pair of worn-out track shoes—excellent for a 100-yard dash, perhaps, but certainly not for the jungle!

"There's nothing wrong with our footwear," I said, "and

we prefer to keep on our coats—that is, if you don't mind."

"Not in the least." He took our bag of provisions and wrapped it up in a large piece of crude rubber of the kind which the Indians have used for thousands of years. "Just tell me when you get tired of wearing the coats," he added. "I'll be glad to carry them. Are you ready?"

We walked past the silent huts of Puyo. Just outside the village the jungle rose like a wall—and Roberto jumped right into it. After a moment of consternation, we followed.

Dawn had begun to break, but in there it was still dark. Several seconds passed before we could even make out the logs which lay across the muddy path at intervals of about two feet, like railroad ties. Then we set out after Roberto in long jumps. I was in a splendid mood. What did the rain matter? It was refreshing; he had painted the devil on the wall just because he wanted to return to his warm bed— just like a mestizo, they're all alike . . . . .

We came to a river, about 180 feet wide. There was no bridge. "Wait a minute," I shouted to Roberto. "How are we going to get across?"

"Like this." He waded out into the water which came nearly up to his hips. When he reached the opposite bank, he turned round and waved to us to follow. I removed my shoes and socks, took Chi-yun on my back, and waded across.

"I wouldn't advise you to take off your shoes every time we come to a river," he said. "It won't be worth the trouble —now that we're in the real jungle."

But I paid little attention to him; I was more worried about getting my feet wet. There were no logs to jump on any more, the path was only a muddy ditch. I tried to walk on the side, but constantly slid down into the middle. Then I tried jumping from side to side, keeping my balance by grabbing hold of overhanging branches. That worked fine —until I clutched a veritable pincushion: a branch covered with sharp spikes. I stopped to pull them out of my bleeding flesh, but there wasn't time for that—Chi-yun was just behind me, and far ahead Roberto's white pants were disappearing into the jungle. I hurried on, still jumping from side to side, but avoiding the branches—I was determined not to wade through the muck in the middle.

Another river, wider than the first one. Stubbornly I took off my shoes and socks, carried Chi-yun across, wiped my feet with my handkerchief, and put them on again. Another fifty yards or so—and yet another river! Fortunately, it was bridged by an old tree trunk. I took Chi-yun's hand and we began to cross, slowly, balancing against each other; but the tree trunk was slippery as wet soap, and I slipped, bringing my wife down with me. There we stood in water and mud up to the waist! I sighed, but at least I had one comfort— now I had no need to worry about getting my feet wet.

"I think I'll take off my coat," Chi-yun said a little later. Though both were guaranteed waterproof, her coat like mine had absorbed several quarts of liquid.

"I'll carry it for you," I said, and was soon staggering under the added weight and gasping with heat. But I was not going either to ask Roberto to carry it, or to take my own coat off—a man has his pride.

Slup, slup, sounded our footsteps. We were wet through from brushing against the branches on either side of the narrow path, for at the slightest touch the leaves released a shower. I unbuttoned my coat. It was wonderful to feel the cool air against my burning body. I took off my coat—my pride was about gone.

I don't remember whether it happened at the twenty-eighth or twenty-ninth river. Roberto stopped at the bank and waited for us.

"I think I'd better carry the *señora* across," he said when we caught up with him. "I doubt whether the *señor* has enough strength to do it."

It was a challenge. I took Chi-yun on my back, and bravely walked out into the current. Gravel and stones were washed away from under my feet—I staggered, reached desperately for a large rock, got hold of it, and hung on for dear life while Chi-yun clung to me. Roberto soon came.

"Hadn't I better take the *señora* after all?" he asked. I clenched my teeth and let him take her. But that wasn't all—without her to weigh me down, my 126-pound frame was like a cork in the water. The current tugged at me; I held onto the rock, not daring to go forward or back.

"Isn't the *señor* coming?" Roberto shouted, when he had crossed with Chi-yun.

"I . . . . . I . . . . ." I was losing my grip. "Please come and carry me, too," I shouted. And thus I crossed the twenty-eighth river—or was it the twenty-ninth?—on the back of a man who was nearly a head shorter than I.

The ground became soggier and soggier. The branches now hung so low that we had to stoop all the time. There wasn't even a ditch any more, only a morass, and we had to jump from the foot of one tree to the next. When we slipped and fell into the mud, one foot would often come up minus its shoe; and you had to pull the shoe out very quickly or the mud would close over it. Once when I stumbled, I hit my head against a tree and crash-landed on my back. Chi-yun screamed.

"What's happened?" shouted Roberto, running back to us. "Has the *señor* hurt himself?"

"No," I replied sourly, rubbing my aching forehead.

"Perhaps I'd better take the coats?" said Roberto innocently.

"Thanks." I avoided his glance. From then on I did not find it quite so hard to move. It now was day; gray streaks of light filtered through the leaky forest ceiling, but we could not see the sky. With the light came the insects. *Moscos,* the worst of them are called. You can't hear them, can hardly even see them, but their bites itch almost as badly as nigua eggs. Each one leaves a dot of blood under your skin. If you squeeze the blood out, you make an inflamed wound; if you don't you will scratch a hole sooner or later and have an inflamed wound anyway.

We had brought along a bottle of American insect repellent. On the label the manufacturers cited four specific reasons why it was superior to all other insect repellents. We rubbed our hands and faces with it and discovered that it had a fifth quality which they had failed to mention—it will blind you in a few seconds. The rain washed the oil down into our eyes, and the smarting was many times worse than the itch.

About seven in the morning we came to a really large river—it was more than a thousand feet wide and bared its teeth in countless places where great stones jutted out of the water. Roberto cupped his hands in front of his mouth and shouted as loudly as he could. Ooooch! The sound was almost drowned by the roar of the river. Again he shouted.

Oooooch! And a faint answer came from the slope on the far side.

"Now we can rest," said Roberto. "The ferryman will soon be here; he has heard us."

My own sufferings had preoccupied me so much that I had hardly given Chi-yun a thought. I took a good look at her and saw that she was wet through and the same color all over—the brownish-gray color of mud. There were a couple of tears in her riding breeches, and her hair hung down over her face in sticky wisps. She sat down on a stone and closed her eyes.

"How are you getting on?" I asked.

"My feet hurt a little, but otherwise I'm all right."

On the opposite bank a canoe shot out into the water. It was grabbed by the current, whirled round twice, and rushed past us, while the man in the stern paddled like mad. He knew how to steer—otherwise the fragile craft would have been smashed against the rocks. In three or four minutes he had covered a distance of more than a mile. Then he steered closer to the bank where the current was not so strong, and laboriously paddled toward us.

Chi-yun was a little frightened; she cannot swim. "Isn't it dangerous to cross the river?" she asked the Indian ferryman. The wrinkles in his brown face deepened, and the black stumps of two teeth became visible as he smiled. "Yes," he answered, "if you're unlucky."

The canoe could take only one passenger at a time. First Roberto crossed. There were several inches of water in the boat, but he lay down flat in the bottom. The point where they landed was so far away that we could hardly see them. The ferryman paddled upriver, crossed, paddled upriver again. Chi-yun gave me a muddy farewell kiss before she crawled in—one never knew whether our luck would hold. I spent some unpleasant moments before I saw the boat land on the opposite bank.

The ferryman thanked me profusely when I paid him one sucre for his trouble. We now stood at the foot of a cliff so steep that it seemed to lean out over us. It could not have been more than a hundred feet to the top, but the path was slippery as ice, and it took us over twenty minutes to get there. Roots would break as soon as we touched them; rolling stones started whole avalanches. When we finally reached the top, Roberto drew a deep breath and told us that now we faced the worst stretch of the whole trip.

The cliffs sloped rather gently toward the jungle, but they were crisscrossed by narrow canyons. You could cross them by crawling over fallen trees, or you could slide down to the bottom and climb up the other side. We preferred the latter alternative, for we thought the trees might not be strong enough to bear our weight. I soon had a hole in my pants, and Chi-yun once made an unfortunate landing in the midst of an anthill whose inch-long inhabitants attacked her furiously.

It was a relief to get back into the jungle. The rain had stopped and the light grew stronger; sometimes we could see patches of blue sky through the foliage. Otherwise, there was surprisingly little to look at—not a flower, not a mushroom, only the same twisted roots, clinging vines, rotting tree trunks, and the green wall of leaves. The jungle is, I think, as monotonous as the sea.

We walked as quickly as we could, but Roberto kept urging us to speed up. The path—or rather the ditch, for it was still full of mud—finally led to a large clearing. Here the head-hunters grew corn, Roberto told us. First they fell the trees, letting them fall on top of each other, and when the soil has dried a little, they sow their corn in between the crisscrossed logs. Then they go away. When they return two or three months later, the jungle is beginning to invade its lost territory, but the Indians are just in time to gather their harvest. When they need corn again, they fell trees in another place; they seldom use the same fields twice. It was the first time I had heard of nomadic agriculture.

This clearing proved to be even more impenetrable than the jungle. Tree trunks lay piled on top of one another, some of them so low that you could not crawl underneath them, others so high up that you could not jump over them. We climbed up and down, gasping in the sunshine. I cut staffs for Chi-yun and myself; they made it easier for us to keep our balance on the tree trunks, but as soon as we returned to the jungle they got stuck in the mud, so we abandoned them.

"Tiger tracks!" said Roberto, stopping and pointing at some tracks in the mud. "They're fresh—it must be a big tiger." (In South America all big, catlike animals are called *tigres*.)

"Are they dangerous?" I asked. Our only weapon was my Finnish boy-scout knife.

"Yes, if they have acquired a taste for human flesh." Roberto looked at Chi-yun. "They always attack the women first, they like their breasts."

At eleven o'clock he wanted to eat. Chi-yun and I were so hot and exhausted that we could not get a bite down, but he consumed, standing, a whole loaf of bread, half-a-dozen hard-boiled eggs, and a huge chunk of goat cheese. Then he hiccuped and licked his chops.

"We should get there in a couple of hours," he said. "But try to speed up a bit. It always rains in the afternoons, and then, as you know"—he glanced meaningly at me—"it's very unpleasant to be in the jungle."

We tried to walk faster, but it was almost impossible—you had to decide beforehand where to put your foot to avoid mudholes, what branch to clutch in order not to fall, where to put the other foot, and so on—and it all took time.

We came to a riverbank completely covered by stones of all sizes. For over an hour we walked along the river. It was torture for our feet, already sore and swollen—we had to jump from stone to stone and, however careful we were, it was impossible not to stub our toes. Perspiration streamed down our bodies and the *moscos* stung diligently; Roberto's legs were covered with tiny dots of blood.

"Another hour at the most." How many times did we hear those words? I don't know whether Roberto said it to encourage or tease us, or maybe he did not know where we were. Anyhow, it went on being "another hour at the most." The path led back into the jungle, and we plodded on, on, and on. "Just one hour more—another hour at the most." It became three o'clock, four, five.

"Hurry up!" Roberto's tone was no longer gently mocking. "If it gets dark, we shan't find them tonight, and there is no place where we can sleep." Even he had begun to look tired.

Half-past five! Roberto was far ahead; we couldn't even hear him any more. It began to rain, not a light rain as had fallen—was it really that morning? We seemed to have spent days in the jungle. The rain sounded like hail on a metal roof; the jungle almost disappeared behind the masses of water streaming down.

The trail divided. We stopped.

"Roberto?"

No answer.

"Roberto! ROBERTO!" We yelled until we were hoarse. By now it was so dark that we could hardly see each other. We sat down on a muddy tree trunk—maybe Roberto would discover our absence and return. I didn't know how long we waited; maybe five minutes, maybe half an hour. Our teeth began to chatter. Chi-yun got up.

"We must go on. Do you hear me, Karl? We'll get pneumonia if we stay here—come on!"

She helped me to get up. I suggested that we follow the path leading to the right. She suggested the other one, and she won. We didn't walk any more, we staggered like drunks. Time and again we fell headlong in the mud. Chi-yun walked ahead and led me by the hand. I thought with hatred of the Holtveds. Yes, they must be mad—only mad people could go and live in this jungle. And I was just as crazy—I had taken my wife along on this journey from which we might never return.

The last thought whizzed round in my head. If we had chosen the wrong path, it was not unlikely that we would perish in the jungle. We could not possibly find our way back to Puyo. Roberto had our provisions, and before long we would have used up all our strength. . . . .

I stopped thinking, lost all identity, became a bunch of flesh and bones which moved mechanically. Time ceased to exist. Even the pain in my feet was no longer there. If

Chi-yun had let go of my hand, I would have collapsed in the mud and stayed there.

"Oh, here you are!" Roberto had to shout to make himself heard above the splashing of the rain. He had been waiting for us for a long time, he said. Why hadn't we kept up with him? It was dangerous for us to walk about alone in the jungle after dark—one risked being killed by the head-hunters.

He cupped his hands to his mouth and hooted like an owl.

"Hoooo—hooo! If you don't do that when you approach an inhabited place, you'll be shot by the head-hunters— you're supposed to warn them of your coming, or they will think you have bad intentions."

We walked on. I fell into a stupor and was aroused a long time afterward by Roberto's voice—"Listen, a river!" I didn't care. Roberto was walking ahead, guiding Chi-yun who in turn was guiding me, and thus we reached the river. Chi-yun and I sank down on the bank while Roberto shouted at the top of his voice. Was it an echo which came back to us? No, it was an answer, weak and distant.

A moment later the rain stopped and the full moon came sailing out amidst bright clouds. We sat up, amazed. Suddenly, the black, menacing jungle had disappeared. The forest was now made of silver—tall, slender trees shone in the dreamy light; the fresh evening breeze made the leaves whisper, and they seemed to tell us that the jungle has many faces, that it can also be beautiful, romantic. . . . .

A canoe grated against the gravel, an Indian ferryman jumped out of the light mist which covered the river. Yes, two foreigners lived a few miles from here, on the opposite bank. He didn't know their names, but they were tall and blond. For a pack of cigarettes he was willing to take us to their house. (The cigarettes were soaking wet, but he didn't seem to mind.)

It was a large canoe with ample room for all of us. We glided along with the current, the Indian only had to steer. After about twenty minutes we pulled up at the right bank, but I could see no signs of any habitation.

"Up on the hill," said the Indian. "It is only a couple of minutes' walk from here."

We climbed the hill and came to a clearing. The house was dark, only its palm-leaf roof shone in the moonlight; it had been built on tall stilts. I speeded up, but Roberto grabbed my arm and again hooted like an owl. "Hoooo—hoooo!" A light appeared in the house. I walked quickly to a ladder leading up to the veranda. Two figures leaned over the railing.

"Who on earth do you think it can be?" a voice said in Danish.

"I'm Danish—Eskelund—Karl Eskelund—I have my wife with me——"

A flashlight shone down on us.

"Good evening," the voice said.

"Good evening—thank God we've found you at last!"

Silence. Why didn't they say something. Did they think we were just passing by?

"I say, couldn't you invite us inside?" I asked with a sinking heart; maybe they really were mad. "We're terribly tired. . . . ."

"Of course, of course—come on up. Welcome! I was so surprised—you see, we've never had any visitors before.

I'm flabbergasted. My wife will be back in a minute—we were in bed already, she's inside putting some clothes on. You must be hungry—I'll heat some food for you right away. I'm afraid we haven't much to offer you, and you'll have to sleep on the floor. . . . ."

Chi-yun collapsed in a wicker chair. It was half-past nine in the evening, and we had been on the go since 5:00 A.M. Later, I found out that we had walked about twenty miles. Chi-yun's ankles were so swollen that I could hardly get her boots off. Her feet were completely covered with blisters; many of them had broken and her socks stuck to the bloody wounds. Three of her toenails were purple. A month later they fell off.

At Home

among

Head-Hunters

HOLTVED LAUGHED WHEN I ASKED WHY HE AND HIS WIFE had chosen to settle down in the jungle.

"We couldn't find a flat in Copenhagen," he answered. "So we came here—there's lots of room in the Oriente."

"Nonsense, Aage!" Mrs. Holtved interrupted. "You know quite well that we came here because we couldn't stand life in Denmark. Everything there was so small and depressing —we longed to be alone with nature."

Aage puffed at his pipe until his long, thin face was almost hidden behind clouds of smoke, as he always does when his wife begins talking about emotions. He is a shy man, tall and with a slight stoop. Frequently he stops in the middle of a sentence; a preoccupied expression comes into his gray, deep-set eyes, and he disappears into a world of his own. How did he happen to marry this impulsive titian blonde who can make a decision with the speed of lightning? How did the dreamer and realist get together?

Because both of them were bored to tears with life in Denmark. Aage had a good position as a schoolteacher, but could find no real satisfaction in correcting compositions and naughty boys. He longed for—but what did he really long for? We can only guess.

If Wilhelmina had not come along and taken him by the hand, he would undoubtedly still be yawning behind the master's desk. She turned his vague longing into a concrete aim—Ecuador. Some ten years earlier she had been to Ecuador with her first husband. They had settled down in the Oriente, but the marriage had proved a failure. After two years they had returned to Denmark and divorced, but Wilhelmina had never forgotten the jungle.

It was winter when she and Aage met—a cold, wet Danish winter. She told him about the sun and the blue sky of South America. While the trams rattled by in the street outside, she described the deep silence of the tropical night. Aage fell in love with Wilhelmina and Ecuador at the same time.

In 1947 they were married and went off. Three months after leaving Copenhagen they arrived at Puyo. For ten dollars the Ecuadorian Government sold them five hundred acres of land which lay near a river deep within the jungle. The two Danes had been urged to settle down in a more civilized district, with white people, but they wanted to get as far away from civilization as possible.

And they did. In Puyo they had to wait for several weeks before they could obtain enough carriers. The Holtveds had brought along some fifteen boxes of tools, guns, ammunition, rubber boots, canned food, and the hundreds of other items which are necessary if you want to build a home in the jungle and remain alive while doing so. The supplies had eaten up all their savings, but they did not intend to bother the grocer for a long time to come.

The carriers were of a different type from the Indians Aage had seen in the highland. Their attitude was not humble or cringing: you soon realized that these Jibaros were free men. They came to Puyo with long blowpipes over their shoulders and a quiver full of darts at their belts. How much were the *señor* and *señora* willing to pay for their help? They didn't want money, but the Holtveds had a large supply of goods for trading. Hour after hour the warriors would sit and study the tempting things. Should they ask for some sticks of dynamite, or a set of shiny fish-hooks, or perhaps a pretty piece of material for the little woman back home at the hut?

Early one morning the caravan finally started—twenty Indians, the blonde woman, and the tall man who was in the jungle for the first time. It must have been a hard trip for him. He was covered with vermin from the filthy hotel at Puyo, and now the *moscos* set upon him. The jungle was unusually wet that year; even at relatively dry spots the mud rose above the ankles. Countless rivers had to be crossed, and the boxes with their supplies mustn't get wet. The Indians seemed to glide over the mud, chatting cheerfully to each other despite the heavy burdens they were carrying. From time to time he had to count the warriors, who loved to run on ahead and then sit down on a tree trunk to wait nonchalantly until the exhausted white man arrived staggering.

The trip took three days. When darkness was about to fall, they would stop at the driest place they could find.

In about fifteen minutes the Indians had built a large, water-proof lean-to of branches and leaves. As soon as they had finished, they would chew a handful of cornstarch and lie down on a heap of leaves. Almost at once they fell asleep; the insects did not bother them.

On the fourth day the caravan arrived at the head-hunters' village a few miles from the land which the Holtveds had bought. There were about thirty huts built on stilts, so it was a relatively large settlement. Close by ran a river, and beyond it lay a Jibaro reservation of many thousand acres where no whites were allowed.

The Holtveds were courteously received by the village chief who let them have a large hut. It took almost a day to clean it out. The two foreigners had to help in catching the parrots which fluttered about under the roof, screeching their protests. There were also five or six monkeys in the hut, besides goats, dogs, chickens, and a tame boar. The head-hunters love animals: one often sees their women suckle some little pet which has lost its mother. When they travel, they take the whole menagerie with them; the monkeys climb about on the heads and shoulders of their owners, the parrots sit on the blowpipes, and the four-legged animals trail behind.

The hut was also populated with another species of animals, so small that they could hardly be seen. Aage had already noticed that the uncombed hair of the head-hunters was full of them. One often sees a Jibaro scratching his head, catching a louse, squashing it between his front teeth and eating it. If he finds a small louse he sometimes puts it back—apparently it must fatten up a bit to suit his taste.

Wilhelmina sprayed the floor and walls with insecticide. (The head-hunters, who disliked the smell, burned the hut as soon as the Holtveds left it.) Then they stacked their boxes in a corner and opened their camp beds.

"It's rather primitive," Wilhelmina had said. "But fortunately we shan't have to stay here for more than a few days —it won't be long before we get our own house."

Nearly four months passed before they did.

The first night they left the door slightly ajar to get some fresh air. About midnight Aage was aroused by something moving on his hand. He felt a large, warm, soft lump and, at the same moment, a stab of pain. When he switched on the flashlight, something fluttered out of the door. It was a vampire bat, and the wound it had made took more than a week to heal.

Later that night they were awakened by rats. The animals gnawed away at the boxes, and one of them ate part of a boot. The rats had the place more or less to themselves, as there wasn't a single cat in the village. The local witch doctor was to blame. All Jibaro witch doctors are fond of drinking a bowl of cat's blood before starting on their religious ceremonies; if no cats are available, a dog's blood is used instead.

Next morning the Holtveds went out to see their land. After an hour's walk they came to a hill a few hundred feet away from a wide river. Here they decided to build their home. They were accompanied by a dozen head-hunters who immediately got busy making a clearing. The natives can do wonders with their long, sharp machetes; by two o'clock in the afternoon the work had progressed so far that a large patch of blue sky could be seen. Then the Indians said, "Enough," for the fishing season was on. They usually fished with hooks or by pouring a pot of barbasco, a plant poison, into the river. A mile or so farther down they would draw a crude net across the river, and collect the dead fish as they came floating along.

But the Holtveds had paid many of the Indians with sticks of dynamite, and now they hurried down to the river, lit the fuses, and hurled the explosives into the water. Some brave men held onto the dynamite as long as possible, and some were so brave that they lost fingers or a hand.

They caught a lot of fish—so many that the occasion had to be celebrated. The next morning they were still drunk, so work had to be postponed until the following day. And the following day it rained. The head-hunters never work when it rains. On the third day they made a good start, but about ten in the morning one of the Indians began to sniff the air.

"I smell tapir!" he shouted. And with cries of joy the others threw down their machetes, grabbed their blowpipes, and ran into the jungle. At two in the afternoon they returned with a dead tapir and two deer, but by then it was too late to resume work, so they celebrated instead. Again they got so drunk they couldn't work the next day.

The Holtveds had ample opportunity to study the village and its inhabitants. They became acquainted with the chief's three wives who all lived in the same hut and apparently lived on friendly terms with each other. When the chief wanted to be alone with one of them, he would disappear into the jungle with her.

One of the women in the village aged about sixteen was better looking than the others, but single. When an Indian visitor arrived, she would usually take a stroll into the jungle with him.

"She is common property," the chief explained when the Holtveds asked about her. The chief knew a little Spanish; Aage was beginning to understand the language and had also learned a few Indian words.

Common property? What did the chief mean?

Well, from the time she became a woman she had shown an unusual interest in men as well as a great ability to please them. It had therefore been decided that she should dedicate her life to serving the other sex. There were times when even a married man needed another woman, and visitors often wanted female company. Her "friends" would give her little presents, but it wasn't strictly necessary.

In many Jibaro villages one finds women who make a living in this way. They never have any children, for the medicine men know all about birth control. Married Jibaro women never have more than ten children; when they reach that number, they go to the doctor and ask for his help.

The medicine man, or witch doctor, makes all his pills and ointments from herbs which he finds in the jungle. The Holtveds discovered that many of his drugs were better than the medicines which they had brought from Europe. He was incredibly dirty and never washed his hands, but for some strange reason the wounds which he treated never seemed to become infected. Of course, he also relied on hocus-pocus: he would spit tobacco juice on the chest or stomach of the patient, mutter to himself, and sometimes he would pull the cause of the pain—a stick or a stone—out of the surprised patient's mouth. The psychological effect was so great that sick people were often cured by the mere sight of the "devil" which had caused all their suffering.

In three weeks the Indians had hacked out a clearing of about five hundred square feet. In the middle they had left a dozen solid tree trunks on which the house was to be built. Naturally, so important a job could not be undertaken without a big feast. The village stood treat and Mr. and Mrs. Holtved were its guests.

The feast took place around a fire on the village square. It began with the serving of cocktails. The glasses were palm leaves twirled into cones, each holding more than a pint. The Holtveds had watched the women preparing the drinks four days before. They had boiled a large pot of yuca, a long root which tastes rather like potato. After cooking it for some time, the women had chewed the yuca into a mush, wrapped it up in leaves, and left it to ferment. Before serving, the mush was diluted with cool spring water. It tasted like beer mixed with buttermilk and was stronger than red wine.

Next, the food was served. There were bananas—boiled and fried with various spices—corn-on-the-cob, corn soup, corncakes, fried tapir and deer, anteater, fish, monkey steak, marsh tortoise, turkey, and parrot soup (the parrot had been boiled for more than twelve hours). The chief treated Aage Holtved to a special delicacy—roasted ants. Headhunters become offended if you refuse to taste their favorite dishes, so Aage shut his eyes and swallowed one that was nearly an inch long. Later he took another, and this time it was not to please the chief.

All night long they feasted and danced while the medicine man beat his drum. The head-hunters drank so much that they had to rest for two days before they could start building the house, and then they did it in their own way. The Holtveds had brought a large supply of nails, but the Indians had no use for them—they tied the beams together with vines and plaited the walls and floors out of tough plant fibers. Slowly, very slowly, the work went ahead. Every third or fourth day they would find something to celebrate—the completion of a floor, or a wall, or the bamboo ladder which was to lead up to the bungalow.

Meanwhile, the Holtveds began to busy themselves with the soil, for their stock of canned goods was almost exhausted. As soon as they moved into their new house, they intended to live off the land and the game in the forest. Aage built a chicken coop and bought a dozen chickens; they planted yucas and bananas and sowed corn and peas. The plants shot up quickly from the rich, black earth which had soon been dried by the sun. When they finally did move in, the yuca bushes were three feet high.

The bungalow had four rooms and a broad veranda running along the entire length of the building. In the largest room was a double bed, a chair, and a table for Mrs. Holtved's toilette things. The veranda was furnished with two hammocks, an oblong table, and half-a-dozen wicker chairs. Beneath the house there was a clay stove.

It was the finest building within a radius of twenty miles. It was also the first real home the Holtveds had ever had together, and they loved it. The whole thing had cost them a little more than one hundred American dollars.

Their first visitors were the termites. On the second or third night, they were aroused by a silent army which was exploring the new house. They were chased out of bed and had to sleep in the hammocks after first soaking the ropes with kerosene. The struggle against the termites lasted several weeks. Insecticide did not deter the busy insects, whose nests were in the forest less than 150 feet away—big, hard balls of clay, branches, and leaves. After experimenting for a while, the Holtveds discovered that the enemy was extremely useful—the chickens were fond of termite eggs, and a chunk of dried termite nest would burn for hours and produce a spicy smoke which kept the *moscos* at bay.

Soon came a new enemy: the coati, a furry animal which resembles a pig and likes yuca root. But the Holtveds soon developed an appetite for coati flesh, and when this thief came to steal vegetables it usually ended in the stomachs of the Danes.

Then came the snakes, crawling by the hundreds to the clearing where they could bask in the sun. This invasion became so serious that the Holtveds dared not climb down the ladder without putting on long boots, for the reptiles would strike if you happened to step on them and many of them were poisonous.

By now the Holtveds had acquired two servants: a young head-hunter and his wife, who came there three or four times a week to help them in the house and the fields. One day the man arrived with two little pigs and tied them to a pole underneath the bungalow. The Holtveds protested: pigs were unclean, and the meat of the wild boar tasted much better.

"But they'll keep the snakes away," explained the head-hunter. He let them loose, and in a few hours they had killed dozens of snakes. It was amusing to watch them—when the snakes struck, the pigs would expose their behinds. The poison could not penetrate the thick layer of fat, and before the snake could prepare to strike again, the pig had broken its neck with its sharp hoofs.

Unbeknown to the Holtveds, angry eyes had been watching them from across the river. The head-hunters who lived there did not like to see the modern world so close to their reservation. The witch doctor in one of the nearby villages was especially disturbed by the presence of the foreigners. He disliked all white people because a mestizo had once sold him a faulty gun. It had exploded and destroyed his right eye. He had never forgotten it. The one-eyed witch doctor had a competitor: a very old medicine man. For many years they had been bitter enemies—they stole each other's patients, and when one of them bewitched a man the other would break the spell out of sheer meanness.

Now it happened that the only son of the one-eyed witch doctor suddenly became ill; he shivered, felt sick, and vomited. There could be no doubt: his soul was bewitched. And who but the malicious old medicine man would think of bewitching an innocent child?

The old man soon heard that he was under suspicion. He did not want to lose his head, so he fled across the river to the village where the Holtveds had lived until they went to their own house. When One-Eye learned of this, he called the warriors of the reservation together, and pointed at his sick son. If they did not put a stop to the old man's evil deeds, all the head-hunters would soon suffer the same fate. However, he had already made a plan which would save them. They were to attack the village across the river, kill its inhabitants and the old medicine man. And while they were about it, One-Eye said, they might as well do away with the two foreigners whose proximity was undoubtedly keeping the good spirits far away from their reservation.

The head-hunters do not make surprise attacks—they always inform their enemies beforehand when they're on the warpath. Thus, the old medicine man and his hosts soon learned that their heads were in danger, and so did the Holtveds. Having no desire for a test of strength with a band of bloodthirsty head-hunters, they sent their servant to Puyo for help.

"Run all the way," they told him, and then they brewed a large pot of coffee and sat down on the veranda, rifles within easy reach. It was a long vigil. They heard drums being beaten in the reservation—the hour of revenge was approaching. Night came; the moon rose. Every sound from the jungle made Aage and Wilhelmina jump. A poisoned dart could so easily fly out of the darkness and find its mark on the veranda.

At daybreak the drums stopped. The head-hunters were on the warpath. Would they come in canoes, or would they cross the river elsewhere and sneak up to the house?

At eight o'clock their servant returned with half-a-dozen soldiers from Puyo. In twelve hours he had covered a distance of more than forty miles! The soldiers made sure that the foreigners were still alive and then went over to the reservation and arrested the one-eyed medicine man. He confessed everything, and the commander in Puyo sentenced him to a year's imprisonment. This was a mere formality, for the authorities take care not to offend the head-hunters, especially the witch doctors. The son recovered, whereupon One-Eye forgave his old enemy. Two weeks later he was released and returned to his village, where soon afterward he opened a school for witch doctors.

Apart from this episode, the Holtveds had no trouble with their neighbors. When we visited them, they had lived in the jungle for nearly a year. The fields had not been enlarged very much, but the banana and papaya trees were bearing fruit, and chicks had become hens which had produced more chicks, and the pigs had killed almost all the snakes. Still, Mrs. Holtved was a little depressed because they had not made more progress.

"It's so difficult," she said. "You just can't trust the head-hunters. 'We'll come tomorrow,' they promise, 'and then we'll get a lot done.' But most of the time they don't come."

"Well, they have their own work to do," Aage put in. "They have to plant corn and yuca, and to go on a head-hunt once in a while—we can't expect them to come and help us all the time."

Mrs. Holtved nodded. "Yes, that's true," she admitted. "It always goes slowly in the jungle. But we live well here, we have peace, and we'll get a lot more done—just give us time!" Eagerly she leaned forward in her chair. "We'll build a new house, a much bigger house . . . . ."

Her husband puffed at his pipe while she described her grandiose plans. She will probably always live in the future, but he is perfectly satisfied with the present—he fetches water from the river, feeds the chickens, and dreams. At times it becomes a bit lonely, he says, but you get used to it. You also get used to the silence and the bites of the *moscos*. There isn't much that he misses from his past—a shrimp sandwich and a cold beer once in a while, that's about all; and he wouldn't exchange the little clearing in the jungle for all the things which the great cities have to offer.

Tsantsas

THE JIBARO INDIANS ARE, I THINK, THE MOST MISUNDER-stood people on earth. We call them barbarians, just because they collect shrunken heads, but in reality the head-hunter isn't very different from you or me. For instance, if you suddenly have a bad pain, what do you do? You go to the doctor and follow his advice. So does the head-hunter. It need not be a physical pain—a nightmare or a fit of gloom is sufficient to send him to the witch doctor's door. In the jungle, death comes from unexpected quarters and often with alarming suddenness, so it pays to be careful.

The witch doctor squats before his door and looks mysterious. Like all doctors he has a particular smell, but in his case it is not a medical odor. He never washes. Greasy, uncombed locks fall down over his face, and around his neck he wears a necklace of human teeth.

"Hmmm," he says when he has listened to the head-hunter's symptoms. "Probably a case of . . . . ." The patient does not understand the last words any more than we do when our doctor speaks Latin. A further examination will be necessary, the medicine man adds and retires to his laboratory, in this case his hut. He may return with a laxative, but it is also possible that he returns empty-handed and stares penetratingly at the patient. "Young man," he says, "the case is even more serious than I thought . . . . ."

He has asked the gods about it, and they revealed the existence of a dangerous enemy—in fact, the man who lives under the tall papaya tree near the waterfall. His soul is trying to do mischief, and if the patient doesn't take preventive measures, he will probably die soon. He doesn't want to die, does he? All right, then he must go into the forest, purify himself, and wait for the signal . . . . .

It's an oral prescription, and the head-hunter accepts it with mixed feelings. Of course, it will be nice to get your soul out of harm's way, but the cure is a damnably troublesome one. First, he must send a message to the man who perhaps yesterday was his friend and warn him of the forthcoming visit. Then, for a whole week, he must live alone in the jungle and not touch meat. Night and morning he has to pray to the gods—and that's only the beginning.

When a week or so has passed, he will hear the witch doctor's drum. The hour has come. With his blowpipe over his shoulder he goes through the forest. Attached to the quiver he has a little bowl of curare, the poison which paralyzes. Even if a fat tapir should cross his path, he may not shoot it; to indulge in such pleasures before he has fulfilled his solemn mission would be blasphemous.

He reaches the hut under the papaya tree near the waterfall. If he is lucky, the whole family is at home and he has a chance of attacking them before they have seen him; otherwise, it's probably the end of him. He kills them all, the father, the mother, and the children. This is necessary, because otherwise their souls might seek revenge later on.

Now he must act quickly, for the souls of the dead are still at large and may play all sorts of tricks before he gets them under control. He hacks off their heads and hurries to a place in the jungle where he has some firewood, some clay pots, and various herbs in readiness. The long shrinking process begins. Until it is completed he must live there like a monk.

When he finally returns, his wife and children run out joyfully to meet him. He is exhausted but feels a little better, thanks to the small, black objects dangling from his belt. The souls of the enemy can no longer harm him. He is their master now—they are just as helpless as the shrunken heads.

The hero does not get much sleep that night. There is a big feast in his honor, with lots of good food and drink. The witch doctor, who is the distinguished guest, bangs away at his drum, telling the happy news to all the jungle: a soul has been liberated!

But quite possibly there is another witch doctor sitting beneath the tall papaya tree and talking to the relatives of the slain. He does not agree with his colleague. "The gods have informed me that the souls of the deceased were pure and innocent," he says. "They have been imprisoned, and they shout for revenge—they must be liberated."

And they can only be liberated in one way: the murderer and his family must share the fate of those he killed. A head for a head, a soul for a soul—that is the law of the

Jibaros. As long as they continue to obey it, there is no danger of the jungle becoming overpopulated.

Tsantsas, these shrunken heads are called. In Quito, it's said that tsantsas with blond hair are often brought out of the jungle, but it's mostly the foreign residents who tell these stories. They flatter themselves. The Jibaros are not in the least bit interested in the heads of foreigners, be they blond or even red. There are exceptions, of course. Thus, it may happen that a white man is paying a visit to a head-hunter, and during dinner the host gets a spasm of pain. It is reasonable to suppose that the white man has caused it, and under such provocation one simply has to take measures against the owner of the vicious soul.

But if the foreigner behaves himself, he will not be killed—and his head most certainly will not be shrunken. It would not be worth the trouble, because white men's heads are not esteemed by the Indians. They think that if the souls of the white men are as foolish as their behavior, they must be worthless.

The Spaniards made several attempts to conquer the Oriente, but always had to give up after suffering heavy losses in endless guerilla fighting. The head-hunters were, and still are, allowed to live in peace. The Ecuadorian authorities make no attempt to tame the unruly children of the jungle. According to the law, it is forbidden to commit murder, but down in the Oriente people still get stomach-aches, kill the originators of the pain, and are in turn killed by the relatives of those they murdered. The government in Quito closes its eyes—officially, there are no head-hunters. It, therefore, seems quite unnecessary to have a law forbidding people to trade in shrunken heads, but there is one. Only if you have good connections, can you get a genuine tsantsa these days.

I bought three from an old Indian in Quito; he came to our hotel early one morning and knocked at the door.

"*Señor*," he whispered when I appeared, rubbing the sleep out of my eyes, "I bring shrunken heads—a mutual acquaintance has sent me hither." The acquaintance is a foreign diplomat who had promised to help me to obtain a couple of tsantsas.

"Come on in," I said. He closed the door behind him and pulled a woman's head, the size of my fist, out of his pocket. She had a wart on her nose.

"It is an unusually fine tsantsa," the Indian assured me. "Look how long the hair is and how firmly the eyebrows remain." He pulled at them to prove his point. "And the eyelashes weren't damaged a bit during the process," he continued. "In Guayaquil this excellent specimen would cost at least a thousand sucres, but I'll let you have it for three hundred."

That was a bit high, I said, pointing out that the skin of the neck had been slit almost to the top of the head; this lowers the value. We finally agreed on 200 sucres. He promised to get me a male head and returned the next morning with a slightly bigger tsantsa which had strong, masculine features.

"He was married to the one you bought yesterday," the Indian told me. "The whole family was killed at the same time—it happened only a few months ago."

I bought the husband, too, and said that I didn't want any more tsantsas, but the following morning the Indian returned. Seemingly deeply touched, he handed me a tiny head. "Now the family can be together again," he said. "This is the son—I'll let you have him for one hundred and twenty sucres."

Kai Arends, the highland truck farmer, is somewhat of an expert on shrunken heads. He told me that they used to be much cheaper. When he worked in the pharmacy in Guayaquil, he sometimes helped his friends to obtain tsantsas from a traveling salesman who sold Japanese goods in the Oriente. One day the salesman suggested that they should become partners. "On my last trip to the Oriente, I learned the secret of the head-hunters," he said excitedly. "We'll grow rich if we work together! I'll mass-produce the tsantsas, and you can sell them—you have good connections."

Arends was both curious and skeptical. "You'll have to prove first that you can really make tsantsas," he said, and the salesman promised to do so. A few nights later he came to Arend's apartment with a big, round parcel under one arm. When he opened it a human head of natural size rolled out on the table.

"Well, I'll be! How on earth did you get hold of it?" Arends asked.

"From the digger at the poor people's graveyard. Now take a good look at it—I want you to be able to recognize it."

Six days later he returned with the smallest tsantsa Arends had ever seen. The skin was black—it always turns black during the shrinking process—and the mouth was sewn up, but it was unmistakably the same head.

"It's almost too small," Arends remarked jokingly.

"That can easily be fixed." The salesman took the head away and returned with it the following night. Now it was almost twice as large as it had been the day before!

How did he do it? The salesman wouldn't disclose his entire secret, but he did give Arends some idea of the process. First, the fresh head is boiled with certain herbs which make the skin swell. The brain, eyes, tongue, and so on are removed. Then the skin is slit up at the neck—as little as possible—and slipped off the cranium. This is the most delicate part of the process; sometimes the bones have to be crushed, and the skin breaks easily. Afterward, the mouth and the neck are sewn up to preserve as far as possible the original shape of the face. The skin—for that is about all that's left—is boiled in a kind of tannic acid which makes it shrink to the desired size. It is then taken out, molded into shape, and smoked rather as you would smoke a ham. The dry heat from the fire makes the skin quite hard.

Arends said that he appreciated the information; but that he had decided, after the most careful consideration, not to accept the tempting offer of partnership. The tsantsa business just wasn't in his line, he felt; he preferred to stick to pharmacy.

They parted friends and met occasionally during the following years. The former salesman established a veritable factory outside the city. The necessary raw materials he obtained from the gravedigger. At that time there was yellow fever in Guayaquil, and when the poor season came —that is to say, the dry season when the fever abated—he made excellent imitations with the heads of monkeys or goats. It was a good business, but in the end the police became suspicious. The tsantsa manufacturer had to flee abroad, and it is said that he eventually settled down in Buenos Aires, a very wealthy man.

Lights
of Lima

ECUADORIANS AND PERUVIANS DO NOT CARE MUCH FOR EACH other, and no wonder, for they have little in common but a stretch of frontier about which they are always quarreling. The struggle is a silent one, fought mainly on the maps of geography books. It centers around a small town, Tumbes, and a large stretch of jungle in the Oriente.

If you open an Ecuadorian school atlas, you'll find Tumbes *north* of the frontier—that is to say, in Ecuador. The Peruvian mapmakers, on the other hand, have placed the town squarely within Peru. But this is a rather insignificant disagreement compared to the one further east, in the Oriente, where the frontier runs completely amuck.

The seed of the struggle was sown more than a century ago when the South American republics were born. In Quito, government specialists procured ancient Spanish documents which clearly proved that Tumbes and the southern part of the Oriente belonged to Ecuador. In Lima, the government possessed documents which were just as aged and venerable, only they proved that both the town and the jungle district were 100 per cent Peruvian.

It was hard to tell who was right. It was not very important, for Tumbes lay in a semidesert, and the southern part of the Oriente was as uninhabitable for white men as the northern portion. The two governments were, therefore, content to fight on the map.

But eight or nine years ago the struggle broke out into the open. Oil was reported to have been found in the Oriente! By then, the Ecuadorians were at least outwardly in control of the disputed areas. Now the Peruvians suddenly resented this. The old Spanish documents were brought out again, and they proved more clearly than ever that Ecuador was entirely in the wrong.

Lima sent an ultimatum to Quito. Would Ecuador willingly give up the loot, or would Peru have to use force?

"If you want the southern Oriente," the Ecuadorians answered, "come and get it!" They probably rubbed their hands at the thought of what the head-hunters and the Aucas Indians would do to the hereditary enemy. Even a strong modern army would stand little chance against the jungle people, they knew.

But the Peruvians knew it too. They now played what the Ecuadorians considered a dirty trick—they hit below the belt, so to speak. Instead of attacking the southern Oriente, as everyone had expected, a mechanized Peruvian force advanced toward the north, along the Pacific coast. It crossed the frontier practically without meeting any resistance, and in a few hours had covered half the distance to Guayaquil.

"Will you throw in the glove now?" Lima asked.

"Yes," groaned Quito, for Guayaquil is the biggest city in Ecuador and has the only good harbor in the country. During the ensuing peace negotiations, the poor Ecuadorians had to cede Tumbes as well as a huge slice of the Oriente. But they never surrendered on the map—in the schoolbooks, the children still see the proud old frontier. And the Ecuadorians say ha-ha, for no oil has been found in the jungle after all!

They're skillful at comforting themselves. Ecuador has some of the worst roads in South America, Peru some of the best. This the Ecuadorians admit. "But," they add eagerly, "good roads are dangerous. Look at the number of Peruvian road accidents! At least ten times as many as here! It's because they don't have any bumps and sharp curves to keep the drivers alert, so they fall asleep. We prefer our own roads."

This way of talking is typical of the Ecuadorians, a carefree, charming, and not very diligent people. The Peruvians, on the other hand, are rather grim and take themselves seriously. You feel it as soon as you cross the frontier. A muddy river separates the two countries; on the Ecuadorian side lies a cluster of wooden huts inhabited by the passport and customs inspectors and a handful of ragged soldiers. You slip the customs officer a little money in order to avoid a thorough examination—at least I did; but then I had a head in my pocket. Chi-yun carried the other two. Whenever we entered another country now, we had to hide the tsantsas and smuggle them across the frontier, for the import of tsantsas is strictly forbidden throughout South America.

Across the river, a small army was drilling on a parade

155

ground. Our passports were carefully examined by an officer with shiny black boots.

"As soon as you arrive at the capital, you'll have to report to the military authorities, the police, and the foreign officer," he snapped. When our luggage had been searched, we boarded a bus and were off. To the left, far out in the distance, we could distinguish the brown wall of the Andes. To the right, the rosy morning sky was mirrored in the Pacific. In between lay a strip of desert which continues all the way down to Chile, and in the middle of the desert ran the road, straight and wide. The needle of the speedometer crawled up to sixty, seventy, and finally stopped at eighty. There it remained. At this speed, I said to Chi-yun, we should soon be in Lima, for the capital was only about nine hundred miles away.

But I had reckoned without the military. Twenty minutes later we were stopped in a village and ordered out of the car. An officer demanded our passports; a nurse wanted to see our smallpox and typhoid certificates. One of the passengers had lost his; he swore that he'd been vaccinated a few days before and showed fresh scars to prove it, but despite his protests he was immediately vaccinated and given an injection against typhoid. We had to wait for half an hour while the officer wrote down our own and our parents' full names, addresses, ages, heights, and other similar information which must have been of great interest to the Peruvian Army. Then we went back to the bus, roared on through the desert—and were stopped again in the next village where the same sort of performance was repeated.

In every town and hamlet, we saw large, red letters on the walls and fences: APRA—Haya de la Torre, Liberator

OF PERU. Sometimes the word "liberator" had been crossed out and replaced by "murderer" or "bandit." These unflattering terms had again been corrected to "leader" or "hope."

What did it mean: *APRA?* Who was this devil or archangel, Haya de la Torre? When we asked our fellow passengers, they looked the other way and pretended not to have heard. We insisted, and at last someone explained that *APRA* was a political party, Haya de la Torre its leader.

Was it a large party? Was it popular? The man didn't answer. Jokingly, I remarked that he seemed afraid to talk about it.

"*APRA* has been outlawed," he said reluctantly. "It's wiser not to talk politics." The others nodded, and with this meager information we had to content ourselves for the moment.

The desert got hotter; alongside the road lay the sun-bleached skeletons of horses and mules, half-buried in the sand. Mirages appeared and faded away again: shady oases with tall, slender palms. Sometimes it really was an oasis—two narrow strips of green on the banks of an almost dried-up river.

Late in the afternoon we came to a riverbed full of strange, oblong pyramids. At first we thought they were sandbanks, but the other passengers said no—some two thousand years ago a great civilization had flourished here. At that time the entire valley was cultivated, and on top of the pyramids lay temples and palaces whose inner walls were covered with hammered gold. The city's name was Chan Chan; by the time the Incas rose to power it was already a ruin.

We drove all night and throughout the following day.

The roads were smooth, the seats soft, yet we could not sleep—the dry heat made the tongue stick to the roof of the mouth, and whenever we were about to doze off, the bus would stop—passport inspection!

The sun was setting when we reached Lima which lies in a broad, fertile valley. The drive through the residential district lasted nearly half an hour. We gaped at the beautiful houses and gardens as if it were another mirage. For a rich Peruvian, a villa in the capital is essential, and they try to surpass each other by building ever bigger and more impressive homes.

Fresh, shady boulevards lead to the center of the city whose attractive churches and dwellings look small and lost among the modern giants of reinforced concrete. Lima is one of the finest towns on the Pacific coast of South America; the slums are not so pretty, but they lie on the outskirts and are seldom seen by tourists.

We had been traveling for more than thirty-six hours. What we needed was an early supper and a soft bed to rest our aching bones—but who can sleep on the first night in a strange town? Lima called with all its glittering lights, so after a quick bath we went out to have a good time. First we had a Chinese dinner, the real stuff, in one of Lima's many Chinese restaurants. Sweet and sour pork, shrimps with asparagus, pigeon—very different fare from what we had become accustomed to throughout the trip. In most of the South American countries, people live mainly on beans, corn, and potatoes, and they can't even prepare such simple food properly. In Peru the potatoes are *frozen* and dried, which makes them keep better and taste much worse. And in Ecuador it is against the law to sell new potatoes—for some strange reason they are believed to be poisonous!

We drank three beers with the food, and the bill came to twelve sol (two dollars). In New York or Hong Kong we'd have had to pay four times as much. Then we took a cab—twenty cents—to the best night club in the city. As we were about to enter, we met two tall men with very long, rust-colored beards, wearing boy-scout uniforms with very short shorts.

"Swedes," I whispered to Chi-yun, and I was right. A moment later, Carlsson and Johnson had introduced themselves and were singing away in their musical native tongue. They had walked and hitchhiked through Europe, Africa, and part of South America, and were now on their way to the States, completely broke but in a wonderful mood.

"People are so kind," Johnson said. "They always give us a ride—but I must say that one encounters some unusual types in between. Last night, when we had just arrived in Lima, we were stopped in the street by a Peruvian gentleman who invited us to his home. He had a nice car and a big villa and gave us a fine dinner. So far, so good, but when we had eaten, he disappeared for a moment and returned with a pair of scissors.

"'I want to cut off your beards,' he said. We thought it was a joke and tried to laugh it off. He smiled and pulled a pistol out of his pocket.

"'I want to cut off your beards,' he repeated, pointing the gun at us. We had almost given up hope, when some servants rushed at him from behind and disarmed him. I think he must have been mad."

Maybe he was—but I will admit that the wild beards

159

also made my fingers itch for a pair of scissors. We now took leave of Carlsson and Johnson; unfortunately, boy scouts were not allowed in the night club.

At first we had the place entirely to ourselves, but about midnight it became crowded with people in evening clothes. Most of them ordered scotch or champagne; we stuck to pisco-sour which was made of native firewater, lemon juice, and white of egg; it tasted fine and cost only twenty-five cents a glass.

Before long an American came over; I had noticed that the people at his table had been staring at Chi-yun.

"Excuse me," he began, "but we've been admiring the young lady, and I hope you won't mind my asking a question. You see, one of my friends insists that she's from North China . . . . ."

He looked inquiringly at Chi-yun, whose smile clearly said that she wasn't in the least bothered by all this attention.

"And I say she's from South China," he went on. "We've made a bet. Who's right?"

"Your friend," said Chi-yun. "I'm from Peking."

"How much did you bet?" I asked the American as he turned to go. Her smile lost some of its luster when she heard his answer.

"A nickel," he said.

Chi-yun, my Chinese wife,
carries water Indian fashion
from Lago de Atitlan,
near our bungalow in Guatemala.

Mei-mei, our daughter,
finds wading in the lake
a happy pastime.

Whether in a bed or hammock, I always write with the typewriter in my lap.

In Guatemala, on the very steps of the churches,
witch doctors perform their magic rites over flaming fires.

This Guatemalan Indian regularly
supplied us with firewood.

The Indians carry wood
or other heavy loads
in this fashion—
a leather band extends
around the bottom of the burden
up over the forehead,
so that the main weight
is supported by the head.

An Indian woman,
dignified but suspicious,
holds her baby,
whose head is protected
from the Evil Eye
by a heavy hood.

Indians gather around the bus we took from Colombia to Ecuador.

Chi-yun rode horseback
when we entered the jungle
in search of
Colorado Indians.

We took this clumsy paddle steamer
up the Magdalena
to reach the Colombian highland.

Chi-yun pauses for a brief rest
on our twenty-mile walk
through the jungle of the Oriente,
from Puyo to the Holtveds'.

Aage and Wilhelmina Holtved
inspect the yuca bushes
near their jungle home.

Mrs. Holtved and a group of head-hunter friends in front of her house.

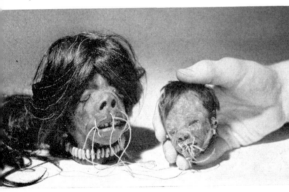

(*Top*) Guanay birds, not humans,
provide high census figures
for Chincha Island.

(*Middle*) Two of the tsantsas
I brought back from Ecuador.

(*Right*) A head-hunter with his blowpipe,
darts, and jar of poison.

Like an eagle's nest, Machu Picchu, the cradle of the Inca people, lies atop a great, steep mountain, some miles from Cusco, Peru.

(*Below, left*) Graceful straw boats float lazily on Lake Titicaca.
(*Right*) A narrow, winding street in Cusco, Peru.

A Bolivian peasant woman,
wearing the inevitable derby,
nurses her child,
while the little girl in the corner
stares at my camera.

Llamas
need not be tethered—
a lasso dropped
around the necks
of two or more
will keep them
from wandering,
for they are too proud
to duck out of the noose,
or too stupid.

In one
of the Peruvian villages
Chi-yun stops
to feed a baby llama.

Saint or Satan

OUR HOSTESS PUT DOWN HER TEACUP SO SUDDENLY THAT SHE spilled some of its contents. She was a distinguished lady, erect despite her sixty-eight years. We could recognize her features in the ancestral paintings on the walls—high forehead, sharp nose, thin lips. I could not meet their glances without involuntarily straightening my necktie.

The old lady belonged to one of the best families in Peru. "You must meet her," an acquaintance had said to us. "She is so typical of the old, noble Peru which, unfortunately, is disappearing."

The tea party had been a most conventional one—until now. We had discussed the weather and the old lady had asked us how we liked Peru. A most attractive country, we had answered, and the cake was very good, etc., etc.

"I'm very interested in the political situation," I had remarked during a lull. "What is your opinion of Haya de la Torre and his party?"

It was then that the old lady had spilled her tea. I won't say she lost control of herself; I doubt whether she ever did that. But her face reddened, her lips tightened, her thin hands shook.

"I won't have his name mentioned in my house!" she exclaimed, but she did not mean it literally, for now she went on. "Haya de la Torre"—she spat out the words—"is the curse of Peru! He has betrayed his country, his class! I'll thank God the day the government gets hold of him and puts him up against a wall—every night I pray for it to happen!"

This sounded promising. A man able to arouse such wrath in an otherwise reserved old lady could not fail to be interesting.

And Haya de la Torre is interesting, whatever else one may think of him. He is an idealist of the most dangerous type—an idealist who doesn't content himself with sitting at home in an easy chair and dreaming. He acts, and his actions are written with blood in the modern history of Peru.

According to our hostess he was an anarchist, Communist, Fascist, homosexual, drunkard, and sadistic murderer. I won't repeat her entire monologue. It was repetitious; when people are angry they tend to go round in circles. I will only repeat the last part of it. In her opinion, it clinched the case against Haya de la Torre.

"His unions have poisoned Peru," she said. "Even the servants at the *Club National*—that's the most exclusive club in the country—even the servants there have had the cheek to organize! And imagine, when we were about to have our Christmas celebration last year, they went on strike! On Christmas Eve, if you please! They wanted higher wages and shorter working hours—but that wasn't the worst of it. They also demanded that their union representative should sit with our board of directors! That a filthy Indian should be in the same room with us during our meeting! I'm convinced that it was one of Haya de la Torre's vicious ideas . . . . ."

About two weeks after the tea party, we were wandering through the ancient ruins outside of Cusco, the former Inca capital. I had cigarettes but no matches, so when I saw a man with a burning cigar, I asked him for a light. It turned out that his English was much better than my Spanish, and we began to talk. He wanted to know where we came from, whether we liked Peru; we asked whether he belonged to this district. No, Trujillo was his home town. Trujillo—didn't Haya de la Torre come from there, too? Yes, he did. Had he ever seen Haya de la Torre? Many times. What did he think of him?

The man—his first name was Jerge—glanced quickly at me.

"Why are you so interested in Haya de la Torre?" he asked.

I explained that I was a journalist and wanted to understand the political situation. For several seconds Jerge was silent. We sat down on a stone throne from which the Inca kings had once reviewed their troops. I noticed that his jacket was frayed at the sleeves. He was a tall man, well built and unusually fair for a Peruvian. I wonder now why he went on to speak so freely to me; I could easily have told the police and had him arrested. But for some reason he must have trusted me.

"I'm an old *Aprista*," he began. "I've been a member of

the party since I was twenty—many a time I've fought for Haya de la Torre, risked my life for him, and I'll do it again when he calls me."

It might have sounded trite, had his eyes and voice not been so serious.

"I'm only a small man within the party," he continued. "But there are thousands and thousands like me. They call us anarchists, but is it anarchy to want to break the chains of the people? The rich have kept us down for hundreds of years, they have kicked us and starved us, but our day will come!"

He rose, filled his chest, and began to sing. The melody was the same as the *"Marseillaise,"* and the echo of his strong voice came rolling back from the gray-stone walls; "Awaken . . . . . fight for freedom . . . . . join the *Alianza Popular!"*

His Adam's apple went on moving after the last verse; I could see that he was trying to restrain his feelings. It must have been a long time since he had sung that song. He sat down and relit the cigar.

"That's our party song," he said. "One day it will be the song of all South America. But you wanted to hear about Haya de la Torre. The first time I saw him . . . . ."

I suspect that Jerge's description of Haya de la Torre was as biased as the old lady's. They were both fanatics on the subject, and so are most Peruvians who can read and write. Under these circumstances, it wasn't easy to form a neutral picture of the leader of the Peruvian lower classes. I did my best, talked to as many people as I could, added a little here, deducted something there, worked out an average, and here is the result.

Haya de la Torre is in his fifties, tall, a bit on the stout side, and has full lips and a dark face. He comes from an excellent family, but his father went broke and young Haya excelled only at drinking and skirt-chasing. No one knows for sure when he began to ponder on the injustices of this world. There was plenty to ponder on in Peru. Most of the country's seven million inhabitants were, and are, desperately poor Indians. Parents will sell their children to get money for food and liquor. *Criaturas,* these slaves are called, and they belong to the purchaser until they are twenty-one; the price varies from fifteen to one hundred U.S. dollars, or more.

The workers in the cities are almost as poor. There is practically no middle class, but a powerful upper class—the people who own the villas in Lima, the mines in the mountains, the great plantations in the river valleys along the coast. Most of them have not earned their riches, but inherited them from their Spanish forefathers who took the land from the Incas. This upper class has ruled Peru for four centuries; first in the name of the Spanish king and then of the republic. Most of the time the army seems to have been in power, for the president is usually an officer, but behind the military dictator stand the rich families.

Young Haya de la Torre ceased drinking and looked about him disapprovingly. Peru's social setup was as unjust as that of France before the Revolution, he said. No one did anything for the poor, who were so ignorant and oppressed that they couldn't do anything for themselves. What they needed was a leader.

He joined one of the small, radical parties which many students flirted with—later on, when they inherited their fathers' money, they usually become staunch conservatives. A short time afterward the party attempted a rather childish revolution. The authorities seized the membership list and de la Torre had to flee abroad.

Now his political education began in earnest. He went to England where, according to his enemies, he was kept by an elderly woman. It is not impossible, for the young Peruvian went out of his way to violate social conventions. He had only one thought: to return to his native land as its savior. Was it because he was ambitious and wanted to revenge himself on the class which had caused his exile? Or did he really feel sorry for the poor? It is hard to say.

He studied the English parliamentary form of government and decided that it was not suitable for Peru—at least not yet. A people must learn to read and write and think before it can rule itself. The Peruvian people were not ripe and never would be as long as the upper classes were in the saddle.

Among his friends were several Communists. He learned a lot from his talks with them. He learned, for instance, that a handful of determined men can seize power and lead a country even though the people are ignorant and apathetic. But he didn't want to join the party. According to his friends, he suspected that once the leaders of the Kremlin got hold of him, they would use him for their own purpose.

Early in the thirties he went to France, and from there to Germany. The contrast between the two countries made a deep impression on him. France was, politically and economically, a sick nation. In Germany, a beaten nation, the Nazis seemed well under way to solving the postwar problems. He admired many of the principles in Hitler's program as well as the thoroughness of the Nazis, but their ultranationalism did not appeal to him.

A short time before his return to Peru he founded *APRA* —*Alianza Popular Revolutionaria Americana*. You don't have to be a Peruvian to belong to the party. It recognizes no frontiers; its aim is to liberate the lower classes throughout South America. First the political and economic chains are to be broken by aggressive Fascist and Communist measures, then the people are to be educated for democracy —at least that's what Haya de la Torre says.

He entered Peru with a forged passport and immediately set about winning supporters for his party. It's surprising how successful he was, considering that he had to work underground. In two years he had started *APRA* cells throughout the country. Practically all city workers were members. Discipline was excellent within the party which had its own flag and laws and punished treachery with death.

Toward the end of the thirties, de la Torre felt strong enough to begin what some call "the campaign for justice," others "the reign of terror." It is said that more than half of the people were for him, and I don't think it's an exaggeration.

A rebellion was organized in de la Torre's home town. Many hundreds were killed before the military became masters of the situation. The rich, who controlled the press, raised a scream of protest against the *APRA* methods. Those who screamed loudest were assassinated.

"Yes, and why not?" Haya de la Torre said when he was accused of being a terrorist. "The rich don't give us a chance. They cling to their privileges and keep us down. As long as we are treated like criminals, we'll have to behave like criminals."

Murders and assassinations were soon the order of the day. The rich stood it as long as they could, but finally they became frightened and gave in—free elections were to be held.

The *Apristas* won and a coalition government was formed: the new party was given most of the civic posts while the Conservatives retained control of the army and the police. Haya de la Torre was the hero of the day. Everywhere he was greeted like a liberator: women shed tears at the sight of him and children threw flowers in his path. But he did not want to take an active part in the government—it was wiser, he thought, to sit behind the scenes and pull the strings.

At first everything went well. New schools were established, unions were organized, wages raised, and the wealthy paid for everything. The poor applauded. The rich said nothing. They waited.

And when some months had passed, de la Torre's followers began to cause trouble. Practically everyone belonging to his party came from the lower classes. They had always been poor; now, for the first time, they had their snouts in the trough, and they couldn't resist the temptation. I don't think they were any more dishonest or greedy than their predecessors, but their sins were advertised with fat headlines.

"*APRA* SCANDAL REVEALED!" shouted the press. "LA TORRE'S HENCHMEN ROB MILLIONS FROM THE PEOPLE! SWINDLES IN LIMA AND SEVERAL OTHER CITIES!"

The newspapers claimed that the *Apristas* had stolen

from the State coffers, and the blushing reformers could not disprove the charge. So they did a stupid thing—they assassinated their bitterest accuser, the editor of one of Lima's leading dailies.

"ANARCHY!" screamed the press, and almost simultaneously a naval revolt broke out at Callao, Lima's port. Some *Apristas* claim that the Conservatives instigated the uprising to get an excuse for seizing power. The Conservatives, of course, blamed Haya de la Torre. Who was lying? I don't know, but 1,400 people were killed in the fighting, and when the smoke cleared away, Peru no longer had a coalition government. The *APRA* was outlawed, many of its leaders were in jail, and Haya de la Torre had gone underground.

At the moment he is living at the Colombian Embassy in Lima which has granted him asylum.* But his supporters have not forgotten him, nor has he forgotten them. Even the most optimistic among the Conservatives are convinced that sooner or later he will make another bid for power. It is unlikely that he will be successful, at least not in the first round, because the army is strong and the *Apristas* have no funds. But he will try again, and the lower classes will follow him. They have no choice, for who else will do anything for the poor? He is their only leader, the only one who gives them any hope. An abyss separates the rich and the poor. On the one side stands a military dictator, backed by the upper classes; on the other, Haya de la Torre, anarchist and terrorist. There is no bridge between them, for in Peru there is no golden mean.

---

* In the spring of 1954 Haya de la Torre was allowed to leave Peru, whereupon he went to Mexico City.

Bountiful Birds,
Naughty Fishes

ALONG THE PERUVIAN COAST LIES A STRING OF SMALL, ROCKY islands. Many of them can hardly be seen from the mainland, but when the west wind blows, you can smell them. Then you hold your nose.

The largest of these islands is called Chincha and has more than four million inhabitants. At least that's what the local commandant says, and he ought to know. His way of taking a census is surprisingly simple. First he reckons how many square yards his subjects occupy, multiplies this figure by five, and then he has the result.

Sometimes, the population swells to between six and seven million. There is neither food nor space for so many, and the commandant might be expected to have to introduce birth control. But nature solves the problem for him. Chincha lies in the Humboldt Current which comes all the way from the seas of Antarctica; in its cool waters live enormous schools of anchovies. They like cold water, but once every five years the temperature in the Humboldt Current for some unknown reason rises five or six degrees. Then the anchovies swim away in search of colder waters, and Chincha, which subsists on the little fishes, is stricken with famine. Rotting corpses cover the entire island; within a few months the population is reduced to two or three million. It's a hard procedure, but the survivors can comfort themselves with the thought that next year the water will become cool again. Then the anchovies return, and with fewer inhabitants there is much more to eat.

Late one afternoon Chi-yun and I went to Chincha. The commandant, warned by cable of our arrival, had sent his private motorboat to pick us up on the mainland. Only after sailing for half an hour or so could we distinguish the island: an insignificant dot in the blue Pacific. Rapidly it grew; we could see fine threads shoot out from the island, flutter softly over the water, then return. A sharp smell of ammonia stung our nostrils. Buildings appeared on the rocks, and before long the motorboat put into a little harbor.

The wharf was crowded with people who waved to us and smiled. In the foreground stood the commandant; he was freshly shaved and was wearing a jacket in honor of the occasion. Deeply touched, I hurried up a swaying rope ladder. I had not expected such a reception; after all, I was only an unknown Danish writer.

It was my intention to greet the commandant with a brotherly Latin embrace; but instead of throwing himself into my outstretched arms, he rushed past me toward Chi-yun, who had just reached the top of the ladder. Bowing deeply, he took her hand and kissed it.

"Señora!" he said. "We thank you for doing us the honor of visiting our island. You are the first woman who has been here for five months. We bid you welcome!"

Eight other men—the commandant's staff—now stepped forward to kiss her hand, one after another. "Lovely!" I heard one of them whisper. "A little piece of heaven!" I received only two very lukewarm handshakes, then they led her away in triumph while the workers remained in the background, still smiling. I wondered why they were smiling, for God knows they got no pleasure except her presence. Later I discovered the truth. They could see her from a distance, they could hear the phonograph music when their superiors danced with her. That was all, but it was enough —the mere thought that a woman was stepping on the same ground as they made them happy.

Chi-yun used no perfume during our stay on Chincha. It would have been a waste, because the ammonia stench neutralized all other smells. It came in overpowering waves from the part of the island where the birds lived. We couldn't see them the first day; darkness was already beginning to fall when we arrived, and the commandant and his men all wanted to dance. It was past midnight when we finally got to bed. For a while we lay listening to the voices of the birds; they sounded like a bass chorus with sore throats. Their voices drowned even the hammering of the waves against the rocks.

Next morning we got up with the sun and walked toward the dark blanket which covered two-thirds of the island. When we approached, we could hardly hear our own voices, so loud was the noise of the birds. They croaked like frogs, grunted like pigs. Our arrival evidently frightened them; a fringe of the blanket fluttered up into the air and we saw that it was white underneath.

So we crept forward on all fours. Slowly the blanket settled down again, and we got to within six feet of its edge.

The nearest bird was an expectant guanay mother. Apart from her white breast she looked like an overgrown crow. She had three eggs in her nest: guanay birds always have precisely that number. If you steal one of them, they lay another. If you steal two, they lay two. But if you take all three, they move house and start all over again. There are limits.

The guanay mother didn't feel at ease in our presence. She rose from her nest, stared suspiciously at us, made a dropping, and settled down again. How many droppings do the birds make? Enough to give Peru every year 160,000 tons of guano, the world's finest fertilizer. There are said to be thirty-five million birds living on all the islands. They are awful gluttons. By dissecting them, it has been calculated that a guanay consumes every day between fifty and sixty anchovies weighing more than two pounds. A pelican eats about five times as much.

When ten minutes had passed, the birds ceased to pay any attention to us. The blanket was in constant motion—birds came flying to relieve their mates sitting on the nests, other birds flew out to get breakfast. They must have had an incredible sense of direction, because there were neither street names nor house numbers, but they always returned to the right door.

Our guanay mother seemed to become weary of waiting for her husband. She rose again and waddled off among the other nests; perhaps she needed exercise. A few steps from

173

her home, she suddenly stopped and filched a feather from somebody else's nest. While she was doing so, another bird ran to *her* nest and stole a feather; and while it was doing so, its nest was raided by a third bird who ran off with a feather. There is a serious shortage of feathers on Chincha during the hatching season, and now thousands of birds jumped up, obsessed by the instinct to plunder. They hissed and hacked at each other with their sharp beaks, beating their wings furiously. Many became so excited that they disgorged undigested fish. Feathers flew; soon the entire battlefield was hidden by a cloud of dust.

And suddenly it was all over—the birds lay on their nests again, puffing and panting. As far as we could tell, the feathers were distributed exactly as they had been before.

So far we had seen only the part of the island inhabited by the guanays; they are the most numerous birds, which is probably why the Guano Islands were named after them. The gulls had their rocky home about a thousand feet away, while the pelicans lived in caves by the water's edge. The different species of birds never live together, and they respect each other's property as well as privacy. That a pelican should steal feathers from a guanay is unthinkable.

Unfortunately, we had little chance of observing the pelicans at close quarters. They were extremely shy and would fly away, however carefully we approached; after a couple of clumsy jumps, they would rise into the air with slow, heavy movements of their wings. They seemed very angry; if they had only worn glasses, they would have looked like my old singing teacher when she was about to give us a scolding.

The gulls were even more sensitive. Although they had

174

built their nests on inaccessible rocks, they would fly off at the mere sight of us. They are the least useful of all the birds on Chincha—they consume an awful lot and deposit their fertilizer on steep rocks where it is out of reach.

About ten o'clock the birds had an enormous meal; a school of anchovies swam close to the island and had to pay dearly for their carelessness. The guanays were the first to reach them; they left the hatching ground in confused masses but immediately organized themselves into long even rows. With energetic beats of their wings they hurried to the school and dived into the water, came up, turned quickly in the air, and swept down again.

After them came the pelicans; they took their time, but could afford to do so, for with their huge beaks they could catch many more fish than the others. Some of them were too greedy, however; on the way back to the island they had to empty their overdistended pouches. The anchovies shone like silver before they disappeared in a white splash.

The gulls were the last to reach the school—they had wasted so much time circling around and screeching. At last the anchovies seemed to realize their danger and retreated deeper into their element.

We returned to the commandant who had many interesting things to tell us. The Spaniards never discovered what riches lay on the islands off their colony, he said; they were too busy digging for gold. Not until the middle of the last century did a German scientist find out that guano is about thirty times more effective as a fertilizer than ordinary stable manure. At that time the islands had accumulated so much guano that they were about one hundred feet higher than they are now, and when the Peruvians finally reached the bottom layers, they found copper spades and shovels of the period of the Incas who had realized the value of the birds' droppings.

The guano industry is now controlled by the government which makes a large profit out of it, as much as four million sol ($240,000) a year. Expenses are low—all you have to do is to shovel the fertilizer into sacks and send it to the mainland. The work is done by Indian laborers from the highland, who get food, lodging, and nearly forty U.S. cents a day. These are excellent conditions for Peru, so there is always a long list of applicants for the jobs.

"They come here on six-month contracts," the commandant said. "In the beginning they stuff themselves like wild animals—it's the first time in their lives they've had enough to eat. At night they sneak out and steal birds and eggs which they cook on the beach. It makes them sick, but we simply can't convince them that they needn't supplement their diet in this way. The digging season lasts six months, and by the time they leave most of them have gained over thirty pounds in weight."

Even the thought of fried guanay made our mouths water, for the sea air had given us ravenous appetites. But lunch proved a disappointment: potato soup and dry cutlets. I asked whether they ever ate fish on the island. Hardly ever. Why not?

"Because—uh—because—" The commandant blushed. "Well, there are scarcely any edible fish in these waters. The only one which tastes good has—ahem—a rather strange quality. It—I must ask the *señora* to forgive the expression—it has an exciting effect. Even if one eats only a little, one has erotic dreams. . . . ."

The naughty fish is called *tramboya,* and of course I wanted to taste it. After lunch I went out in a small rowboat. I fished with a line, using anchovies as bait, and within forty minutes I had caught twenty-three *tramboyas* of over a pound each. Chi-yun and I couldn't possibly eat them all, so we persuaded our hosts to assist us, which they somewhat reluctantly agreed to do. Dinner consisted of *tramboya* soup and fried *tramboya.*

"Did you sleep well?" was the radio operator's first question when we appeared for breakfast the next morning. I usually had nightmares, I told him, but that night I had slept like a stone. Chi-yun had no recollection of dreams, either.

"And how did *you* sleep?" I asked the commandant, who was also present.

"Will you please pass the salt," he said, turning purple in the face, and during the rest of our stay on the island he scrupulously avoided meeting Chi-yun's glances.

Where
the Dollar
Lasts

NEAR THE MAIN SQUARE OF AREQUIPA THERE IS A CHURCH
which American tourists invariably photograph. Not that it
is a beautiful church. Built of gray volcanic stone, it
resembles an enormous barn, but the entrance is ornamented
with the statues of two naked women in bas-relief. It's these
statues that attract the amateur photographers, and they
certainly are original; their breasts have been sawn off.

The operation took place more than a century ago, when
a new bishop had just been appointed to Arequipa. The
precise motive for his action is unknown, but it is assumed
that the swelling bosoms caught his glance whenever he
entered the church. At last he could stand it no longer, and
he ordered the offending objects to be removed. The desired
effect has not been achieved, however, for the girls seem
naughtier than ever—their lack of breasts immediately fires
the imagination. But the Bishop undoubtedly had the best
intentions imaginable.

178

The second of November is the priests' busiest day in the year. It is called "All Saints' Day," and from early morning people stream to the graveyards. Here, the earthly remains of the rich rest in splendid marble vaults. The doors are opened, the bones carefully cleaned with alcohol or Eau de Cologne. This is said to please the saints. The poor lie buried in another part where there are no marble vaults, only modest little heaps of stones. Their bones cannot very well be taken out from the graves, so the mourners merely whitewash the stones.

The priest rushes about with a cross in one hand and a box of matches in the other. At each grave he stops and, on receiving a small cash payment, lights a rocket. People cross themselves as it shoots up into the air. If it goes straight, it means that the soul of the dead is already in heaven; if it goes sideways, the poor sinner is still suffering in purgatory, and then the priest must say masses.

Arequipa owes its name, perhaps its very existence, to the Inca kings. They were very fond of fish. Daily, relays of runners brought baskets of fresh sea food from the Pacific Ocean to the royal table in Cusco, Navel of the World. The first part of the road back to the capital led through a burning desert. The runners passed a river which came from a nearby mountain and emptied itself into the sand, and here they often felt like refreshing themselves with a bath. At last one of them had the courage to ask the king whether they might take a short rest on the bank of the river.

"Are Quepay," answered the king—yes, rest.

The place where they rested became an oasis. It was often visited by the Inca kings, for nearby were hot springs, said to have healing powers. They are still very popular. Chi-yun and I visited one of them, which is believed to be the same one where the Incas bathed. It has changed quite a bit since then: the water now comes bubbling up into four cement pools. The first pool is for those suffering from diseases of the eyes, the second is for people with liver trouble, the third for those who have rheumatism. And the fourth one, said the caretaker, contains mixed water and is for busy people who want all the benefits in one quick dose.

In Arequipa, you probably get more for your U.S. dollars than anywhere else in the world. We met an old American acquaintance who had settled down in the city with his wife and daughter. They lived like kings with a modern villa, four servants, plenty of entertaining, and much whiskey—and their total expenses amounted to a hundred dollars a month.

For this they can thank the dollar shortage. The official exchange is about seven sol for the dollar, but you actually get seventeen or eighteen. A worker makes four to eight sol a day, so a greenback will really get you places. We lived at the best hotel in the town and paid three U.S. dollars a day for the two of us, food included.

Gold was so reasonable in price that I felt obliged to buy some jewelry for my wife. First she chose a heavy bracelet, then she fell in love with a pair of antique filigree earrings adorned with little pearls. I don't much care for earrings, but there's one thing I dislike even more: painted fingernails.

"I'll let you have the earrings," I said, "if you'll promise never to paint your nails again."

A silent struggle took place in Chi-yun. In the end, the earrings won. Now she had to have her ears pierced, and the cook at the hotel where we lived offered to do it for her.

I suffered much more than Chi-yun. It looked awful—the needle wouldn't go through and there was blood all over the place, but she smiled calmly throughout the operation. The cook left a thread sticking through each earlobe. A week later Chi-yun removed the threads and put on the earrings, although the wounds were still not quite healed.

When shortly afterward we went for a walk, I noticed that my wife was the object of even more stares than usual; some street urchins even whistled at her. We couldn't understand why until we returned to the hotel where an American woman told us that Chi-yun really must not wear those earrings out of doors—only Indian girls of somewhat doubtful reputation did so. But Chi-yun did not care and continued to wear them.

The owner of the hotel, *Tia* [Aunt] Bates, is a small, lively lady in her eighties. Whether she is English, Scotch, or American is a question which puzzles her guests. She won't tell, and her accent is a queer mixture of all three. She has white hair, determined lips, and quick, blue eyes which manage splendidly without the aid of glasses. Her memory has never been good; two years ago she left a young American couple in charge of the hotel while she went on a trip to the States, and a month later she wrote to them, to ask how they were doing. "By the way, I would like you to write and let me know your names," she concluded.

The guests tremble when *Tia* is in a bad mood, for her sarcasm is equally biting in English or in Spanish, but she really has a heart of gold. At the beginning of the century, when she arrived in Peru, she was married to an Englishman. He was obsessed by the thought of finding gold and eventually ran away from his wife and children, leaving only debts behind.

Twenty years later he returned. He had found no gold, only disappointment and poverty, and in the meantime his wife had built up one of the best-known hotels in South America—you just don't count as a world traveler if you have not stayed at *Tia's*. She never reproached him with a single word, but built a bungalow for him in the hotel garden, and here he lived happily until the end of his days.

There can be no doubt that *Tia* will go to heaven when she leaves us. The natives love her, and when an Indian baby dies, its mother often comes and asks *Tia* for a long ribbon. Everyone knows that the innocent little ones go straight to God, and as soon as *Tia* dies all the children will pull away at their ribbons and drag their dear auntie up where she belongs.

From Arequipa we took the train to Cusco. I had always connected the Incas with sunshine and warmth, and wondered why they built their capital on the dour highland. The air is thin and cold in Cusco; icy winds blow down from the mountains and howl through the crooked streets of the little town. Of all the living things there, only the llamas seem to be able to resist the cold. You see lots of them on the plaza, well protected by their thick fur coats. No need to tether them: all you have to do is to make them stand in a circle, as in a football huddle, and then put a lasso round their necks. They could easily get away by dipping their heads and backing out, but the llamas are too proud to do that, or maybe too stupid.

Cusco made us think of a graveyard where the corpses haven't been properly buried. Everywhere you see the bones of the dead sticking up—the ruins of the old Inca temples and palaces. They were torn down by the Spaniards; only a few walls resisted the hammer and chisel so stubbornly that they were permitted to remain.

The Temple of the Sun was the hardest nut to crack. Its walls, more than three feet thick, were built of giant stones. Using no mortar, the Incas fitted them so neatly together that not even a knife blade can be thrust between them. When the Spaniards had succeeded in destroying about three-fourths of the building, they grew weary and built a church and a monastery out of the remains of the holiest of all Inca temples. Inside the latter you can still see several rooms belonging to the Inca period. They have clear, beautiful lines, and in one of them there was a large bas-relief of the sun, made of the purest gold. When you leave this chamber and enter the church with its multitude of garish saints, you feel no enthusiasm for the victory of the cross over the heathen.

It is hard to believe that at one time Cusco had two hundred thousand inhabitants and was the capital of an empire as large as Europe without Russia. Today it is a sleepy little town with a population of less than sixty thousand. Cusco has declined since the conquest, and so, in a way, has all Peru. At one time this country fed more than fifteen million diligent people who had an admirable social system.

The present-day population is only about eight million, and they cannot even feed themselves—Peru must import large quantities of foodstuffs from abroad. Few would use the word "admirable" with regard to the present social system of Peru. Why? In Colombia and Ecuador I had often asked myself the same question, and later on it was to turn up in Bolivia. All these countries have almost unlimited possibilities. Why are they so poor and backward?

"It's the fault of the Indians," say the whites. "They are so lazy and unreliable—it would be best to castrate the lot of them or exterminate them in some other way. They're the ones who hold us back. . . . ."

Is it true? I doubt it, for I have visited Machu Picchu, the cradle of the Inca people. The Spaniards never found Machu Picchu, and here one can see what the useless Indians were capable of doing before the white man came.

Machu Picchu

LIKE AN EAGLE'S NEST MACHU PICCHU LIES ATOP A GREAT, steep mountain. Around the foot of the mountain a river foams in a semicircle. Urubambá is the name of the river, and when you stand on its bank and look up, it is just possible to distinguish the outer wall of the dead city. You feel as if the whole mountain were toppling down on top of you—that is because the clouds are moving, the gray, heavy clouds which come floating endlessly from the Amazon Valley toward the east.

An Indian can climb the mountain, but tourists are wiser to hire mules. The thin legs of the little animals are much more reliable than your own on the muddy path which zigzags until your head begins to swim; in some places it is barely a foot wide. As you climb higher up, the Urubambá becomes smaller and smaller, and its thunder dwindles to a monotonous murmur. A stone torn loose by the mules will start an avalanche which lands in the river with a

185

tremendous splash. Machu Picchu can no longer be seen; the rocky mountainsides towering above you seem perpendicular. After half an hour's ride you arrive at the hotel, wet with perspiration, although the air is cool up here.

Chi-yun and I took a room and signed our names in the guest book. Visitors from all over the world had been here and written down their impressions with plenty of exclamation marks. One man didn't seem to have been very impressed. "Machu Picchu is okay," he wrote, "but have you ever been to Texas?"

We left the hotel and began walking along a narrow path. It was late in the afternoon; most of the Urubambá Valley was already hidden beneath the evening shadows. We came to a sharp turn of the path, and stopped. Before us lay a scene of breathtaking beauty: a great city which seemed to be part of the very mountain. You couldn't tell where the rocks ceased and the gray stone walls began. Towers and palaces clung to hillsides so steep that you would have thought it hardly possible for a man to get a foothold. Among the buildings lay hundreds of terraces, regular as stairways.

As we continued, the sun found a hole in the clouds and threw a white beam down upon the city. We climbed up one of the numerous staircases which ran between the rows of buildings. There were many steps, so many that we tired of counting them. Finally, we reached the top of the mountain and stood on a great plaza surrounded by tall buildings. This had once been the holy square of the Incas, where the people gathered for religious ceremonies and occasions of state; here they had probably listened to the last speech of their king before they set out to conquer the world.

Above all the other buildings, even above the king's palace, towered the Temple of the Sun. We walked past the long, broad altar; now we could see the other half of the city which lay on an even steeper slope. Just to look down made you dizzy. Many of the terraces were no larger than the floor of an ordinary living room, with the next terrace ten or twelve feet below. It must have taken many, many years to build the strong stone walls which prevented these tiny fields from sliding down into the Urubambá Valley.

The outer wall begins some two thousand feet below the Temple of the Sun and encircles the city in an uneven ring. Just inside the wall are the military barracks: broad, squat buildings with lookout points from where the watchful eyes of the guards could follow every move of an enemy daring enough to attempt an assault on the fortress. Above the barracks lay the dwelling places of the people: plain stone houses once topped by straw roofs. Then came the inner wall above which lived the priests and the royal family.

In the whole city there are only three windows; they pierce the western wall of the Temple of the Sun and are so large that a grown man can almost stand erect in them. With hollow eyes they stare across the Urubambá Valley, toward the remote Cusco plateau—perhaps they were symbolic of the Inca *Drang nach Osten*.

The Incas had good reasons for building their city in a place so remote and inaccessible. It is believed that about two thousand years ago Peru was invaded by barbaric tribes from the cold south. All the existing civilizations in the country succumbed to the wild hordes—all but a small group of people who, after a long flight, came to this spot, then a barren mountain. They probably rolled boulders down on the pursuing enemy and thus halted him. The construction of the city—the complete lack of any gates—support the contention that its inhabitants lived under a constant state of siege and hardly ever dared to go down into the valley.

When carefully tilled, the terraces could support between fifteen hundred and two thousand people. Machu Picchu was not discovered until 1911, and later on the ruins of three or four similar cities were found on mountaintops in the surrounding district. The population of the mother city must have built them for lack of sufficient food or space.

The fortress people probably didn't get much to eat except corn, a few vegetables, and the meat of llamas. They wove their clothes of llama wool and used llama dung for fuel. Their greatest fear must have been that the barbarians might try to cut their water supply, but fortunately the main spring came from a nearby peak which was even higher and more inaccessible than Machu Picchu.

It is easy to imagine how the brilliant collective system of the Incas was born in the beleaguered cities. It was almost inevitable. The individual was not allowed to own land, for it was of such vital importance to the existence of the community. It belonged to all. The fields were jointly cultivated, the harvest was divided into as many shares as there were mouths. The wool, the llama dung, the water, the work— everything was shared. There were no special rewards in the form of higher pay for those who made larger contributions, and it probably was not necessary—the Incas seemed to get along well without "private initiative." Money was unknown, but everyone received his due. "One for all and all for one" was the motto of the Incas, and they really carried it out.

188

But human beings must have something to look up to, something which is bigger than themselves. In the Inca cities it was the chief. Perhaps he was elected in the beginning, but later on the priests decided that it was wiser to give him a certain relation to the source of light and warmth, the greatest power in the universe. When it comes to religion, the common man will believe in the fantastic rather than in the plausible. Priests have always known this, which doubtless explains why most religions, originally pure and sensible philosophies of life, later become embroidered with miracles and mysterious ceremonies.

The chief, declared the priests in the Inca cities, was the Son of the Sun. Therefore he was different from ordinary men, so he must be given a castle to live in and a splendid headdress of multicolored plumes. When the people prayed to the sun, they also prayed to their king, for now they were one and the same.

The Incas were isolated on their hilltops for about a thousand years. Then they felt strong enough to come down and reconquer the world which their forefathers had lost to the barbarians. There were probably no more than five thousand, women and children included, but every man was hardened, able, and incorruptible.

As far as is known, Cusco was one of the first large cities which the Incas captured. They immediately started to organize the people on the lines of the social system which they had developed in their mountain strongholds. Everything was confiscated: from now on there was no private property. The State undertook to feed and clothe its subjects—and it did. The defeated tribes discovered that life was pleasant under their new rulers. Their masters were

189

severe but just. If a man fell sick and could not work, he would still receive food and clothing; if children lost their parents, they were brought up at the expense of the state. All men were conscripted for a certain number of days of the year to build terraces and hew stones for fortifications, and they also had to join the army for a set period.

When the social structure of the Cusco area had been recast according to the pattern of Machu Picchu, the Sons of the Sun went forth to bring the light of civilization to the heathens in the surrounding territories. It must have been comparatively easy for them to persuade their neighbors, for the Inca soldiers were armed with murderous clubs and had great skill in crushing heads. Defeated chiefs were brought to Cusco, given palaces to live in, and treated with every respect. At the plaza in the center of the capital there was a garden with beds containing earth from each of the conquered districts. Soon there were so many beds that it had to be enlarged.

The empire was now nearly as large as present-day Peru, and it was ruled exclusively by the men from the eagle's nest and their descendants. They formed a kind of nobility —they were Incas. But they were not permitted to rest on their laurels. The slightest deviation from the line of duty was instantly reported to Cusco, and erring officials were punished much more severely than the common people. Once a year the Inca king journeyed through the country on a golden litter, and anyone could complain to him if the local Inca representatives had been unjust.

Roads were built; even today you can follow their traces from the Colombian border down to southern Peru. Daily the country was crossed by royal runners who carried little sticks with colored strings tied to them. The written word was unknown, but by letting his fingers run over the knots in these thongs the Inca immediately knew what the sender of the message had to say.

Cusco grew. From the defeated people the Incas had learned how to procure and to work gold, and they adorned their temples and palaces with the yellow metal. "Tears of the Sun," they called it—it was pretty to look at and holy because of its supposed origin, and apart from that it had no value. The king wore golden ornaments on his chest and knees, the walls of the Temple of the Sun were decorated with gold, and in the park outside the temple stood golden replicas of plants and animals.

The dead Inca kings and their closest relatives were embalmed and kept in a large, dimly lighted hall where they sat in lonely splendor on their thrones. Once a year they were dusted, placed around a large table in the royal palace, and served a big dinner on golden plates. When they had looked at the food for a while, they were returned to the hall of the dead.

Three hundred years after the arrival of the Incas in Cusco, the empire had grown until it covered a stretch of nearly three thousand miles along the Pacific. Only the head-hunters in the Amazon Valley and the Arauca Indians in central Chile had been able to resist the Inca armies which now numbered several hundred thousand men. It is not improbable that the entire continent would have been conquered within the next few centuries.

But fate had other plans for the Children of the Sun. One day some three hundred bearded adventurers landed close to the present frontier between Ecuador and Peru.

After a long march they arrived at a mountain resort where the Inca king, Atahualpa, had his temporary headquarters. On his orders, the Spaniards were given a place to stay: a large, square building with a courtyard in the center. Atahualpa was curious to see the hairy people who rode on strange animals and produced thunder and lightning from long sticks, so he accepted when Pizarro invited him for a visit.

"Come without arms," Pizarro said. "We will meet like brothers."

The Inca king came unarmed, carried on his litter, and surrounded by more than a thousand officials and servants. All the Spaniards had weapons hidden under their clothes. When the natives had all entered the courtyard, the gate was closed behind them. Still they were not suspicious. A monk stepped forward and handed Atahualpa a Bible. The white men came on behalf of their king, explained the monk through an interpreter, to tell the people of this country about the Holy Trinity.

"We Christians worship three gods and one god, and that makes four gods," he said according to the historical reports. He added that Atahualpa must submit to the Spanish king and worship the one and only god of the Christians.

The eyes of the Inca king flashed. He threw the Bible to the ground and ordered his people to carry him away, but at that moment the Spaniards attacked. Practically all Atahualpa's attendants were slaughtered. Only one Spaniard was wounded—it was Pizarro, who received a cut on his hand when he raised his arm to prevent a soldier from killing the Inca king.

Atahualpa was now the prisoner of the Spaniards, who

promised to release him if he would fill a large room with gold. When his faithful people had almost carried out this condition, the white men killed him under a trumped-up charge. At first they wanted to burn him alive, but at the last moment he agreed to be baptized, and as a reward he was permitted to be strangled instead.

With him died the empire—the Incas paid the penalty of overcentralization. The people were paralyzed without him. There was no one to give orders, and the armies suffered one defeat after another although they fought bravely. Cusco and all the other rich cities were plundered. There were few crimes which the Spaniards left uncommitted in their blind desire for the Tears of the Sun.

The brilliant social system of the Incas collapsed within a few years. The terraces fell into ruin—the great terraces whose remnants can still be seen throughout Peru and Bolivia; they are as impressive as the Great Wall of China. The Indians were used as slave labor. I have been down in one of the old Spanish mine shafts. It zigzagged to a depth of more than twelve hundred feet; I had to crawl on all fours, and when I had covered a fourth of the way down I felt as if I were being choked. I clenched my teeth and continued, but after another hundred feet or so I couldn't take it any more. The fresh air was like wine when I stepped back into the light.

In such rat holes the Indians had to work from twelve to fourteen hours a day. The Spaniards had taken everything away from them, even their right to live as human beings; and here we find the answer to the question: Is it the Indians who retard the development of countries like Peru and Bolivia?

"The Indian is a lazy, unreliable drunkard," say the whites. Yes, it is true—firewater was his only comfort during all those years when he sank ever deeper into poverty and wretchedness. Now the whites suddenly demand that he should develop into a useful and industrious citizen; but the Indian raises his bottle of *aguardiente* and takes a big gulp. That is his answer. For nearly four hundred years he was treated like an animal. He became an animal, and so far no real attempt has been made to change him back into a human being.

In a way the Spaniards suffered from their own actions. They had come to find gold. They found it, they conquered a world. But they didn't know how to build, only how to destroy. They added nothing to the culture which they found; they crushed it and bled the people. Slowly their energy left them because they had slaves to do everything for them. They despised the Indians; their conceit grew and later developed into the extreme jingoism to be found today among most of the descendants of the Spaniards in South America.

Yet, it is impossible to blame entirely the whites, or the Indians, or the mestizos for the present stagnation of these countries—the only too apparent halt in their development. Who is to blame, then?

It would be interesting to take an Indian, or a mestizo, or a white South American and bring him up in, say New England. I believe that he would grow up to be an average American child, without any of the unfortunate characteristics such as unreliability and incompetence, which so many associate with the Latin Americans. These traits are not innate. They are the natural result of the Spanish colonial system, a system which destroyed master and slave alike. The pillars of this system still stand firmly established, and as long as they are permitted to remain, Latin America will continue to reap the bitter harvest which the Spanish conquerors sowed.

Chi-yun Wins

IF IT HAD NOT BEEN FOR THAT LLAMA, WE WOULD UNDOUBTEDLY have taken the train to Bolivia. Chi-yun had practically persuaded me. "Don't be so stubborn," she said. "The train is much faster and much more comfortable than a bus. Besides, I'm sick and tired of buses, and I've just had my hair washed. . . . ."

She gasped for breath; we were nearly twelve thousand feet above sea level in a small Peruvian village not far from the frontier. From the snow-covered mountaintops, half-hidden beneath lead-gray clouds, came cold gusts of wind. In the distance we could make out a narrow strip of Lake Titicaca, the highest navigable stretch of water in the world.

"But I shan't get any material that way," I protested. "I want to write about the Indians, and I'll bet you they can't afford to go by train."

"Why don't you walk all the way then?" Chi-yun asked sarcastically. "The Indians certainly can't afford to go by truck, either—as a matter of fact, I doubt whether it's much cheaper than the train. . . . ."

She stopped, frightened by a low hissing—a tall, brown llama had sneaked up to us while we were talking. Contemptuously, it showed its yellow front teeth in a sneer and spat again. It didn't hit us this time, but Chi-yun grabbed my hand and began to run. Someone had once told her that you can get a social disease from llama spit; I had, of course, assured her that it was nonsense, but she was not quite convinced.

"Take it easy!" I said. "Llamas are perfectly harmless." I was secretly pleased, for the incident had suddenly changed the situation—now I was the strong man, she the helpless little woman.

"Of course the train is more expensive," I continued. "The tickets cost forty dollars [we always estimated prices in U.S. dollars] with sleepers. I'm sure we can do it for less than half that price by truck, and we've really been spending too much money lately."

Half an hour later we sat on the front seat of a bouncing truck, heading for Lake Titicaca and Bolivia. On top of our luggage, which was at the back of the vehicle, stood and sat some thirty Indians.

"Do you suppose we'll reach the border before dark?" I asked the driver. It was not an unreasonable question, for we were less than thirty miles from Bolivia.

"Yes, if you pay me a hundred sol [$6.00]," he answered. "Otherwise, we won't," he added without even a blush.

"A hundred sol," I said, horrified. "Certainly not!"

He shrugged and slowed down a bit, just to show me who was master. We crawled along the shore of the lake—

I could have counted up to two thousand between each milestone. From time to time we would stop to pick up another Indian. The other passengers protested angrily, whereupon the driver gave them a thorough tongue-lashing, which never took less than five minutes. Chi-yun felt sore from sitting down for so long, but refused to go outside when we stopped—quite sensible of her, for shyness was unknown to these Indians and one risked being hit by a spray from above.

Titicaca cannot fail to inspire you: a tremendous expanse of blue water surrounded by great mountains which are scarred by the ruins of Inca terraces. But there's so much of it—nearly a hundred miles, and when you have seen the first ten you have seen it all. We were fed up with the lake when, at six-thirty in the evening, we finally reached the frontier town. I have forgotten its name, but it left other memories, the thought of which makes me itch all over.

We wanted to cross the frontier that same evening. Impossible, said the driver; the nearest Bolivian village was eight miles away and the customs had already shut their doors. We would have to spend the night here, but if I gave him sixty sol ($3.60) he'd take us across the frontier early next morning in time for us to catch the bus to La Paz.

I tried to make him reduce the price. Nothing doing, so I went to the town square and approached a group of Indians. Would two of them carry my luggage across the border early next morning? Yes, there were two who were willing to help me, but the question was: How much? Warily, we avoided committing ourselves: "It's a long and hard journey," the Indians pointed out. "We'll have to get up before dawn, and the mornings are cold. It's doubtful whether *Señor* can find any others who will even consider doing it. . . . ."

In the end their patience proved greater than mine—when it had grown dark and the rumbling of my stomach threatened to drown my own voice, I broke down and offered them fifteen sol (ninety cents) apiece. It must have been far too much, for they agreed without any hesitation.

In China I have slept at hotels which were worse than the one where we spent the night, but not much worse. The toilet was a yard behind the bedrooms; you went there with a flickering candle in one hand, a stick in the other for defending yourself against a gang of snarling dogs; so you couldn't hold your nose however much you wanted to. Our small room was furnished with two, narrow, wooden beds and a picture of the Virgin Mary. We used only one of the beds, and to avoid freezing too much we lay so close together that neither lice nor fleas could squeeze in between us. They concentrated their attacks on other parts of us, seemingly hog-wild after the shot of DDT which we had given them a little earlier.

The two Indians had solemnly promised to fetch us at four in the morning. Of course, they did not; but I knew where they lived, so a little after four I went out in the cold night to get them. I had to kick the door several times before a grunt sounded from inside the clay hut. A woman came and let me in. Our bearers had evidently celebrated the prospect of earning thirty sol; both were unconscious and their breath told why. The woman shook them violently, and after several minutes one of them staggered to his feet.

"You'll have to awaken the other one, too," I said. "One man can't carry all the luggage."

"I help," said the woman, pointing at herself. She had already put on her bowler hat. (All self-respecting Indian women in these parts own a bowler hat.) I don't think she weighed over a hundred pounds, but she had the strength of a mule. They divided our luggage—two suitcases, a bag, and a typewriter—between them, and we went out onto the pitch-dark road. Before long our hearts were hammering; you can't stand much exertion at such an altitude, and the road was climbing most of the time. Chi-yun's nose bled, but I didn't know this until daybreak.

The new day began to dawn; now we could see the outlines of the lake and the mountains. With bated breath we sneaked past the guardhouse of the Peruvian border patrol. A ten-minute walk through no man's land brought us to Bolivia. Again we passed the frontier guards whose snoring we could hear from inside a hut, and we smiled to each other in the gray light—for the first time in twelve years of traveling we had crossed a border without the blessings of customs and passport inspectors.

By the time the sun rose we had arrived in Copacabana, the Bolivian border town. Instead of the promised bus we found a truck packed with Indians. Fresh air may be healthy, but the prospect of standing at the back all the way to La Paz was far from pleasant. After a short argument with the driver, we agreed to pay four times the usual fare for the privilege of sitting next to him in front.

Again we drove along the shores of Titicaca, hour after hour. We saw the straw boats of the natives floating gracefully on the water; after each trip they had to be pulled ashore and dried in the sun. About seven in the evening we arrived at La Paz, tired and dirty.

"I hope you enjoyed the trip," said Chi-yun, and her tone was not pleasant. I wanted to prove to her that at least it had been cheap, so I immediately began doing the account. It wasn't easy—first I changed the Peruvian sol into Bolivian money, which I again changed into U. S. dollars.

"Well?" said Chi-yun when she saw me staring at the final figure.

"Forty-seven dollars," I muttered without looking at her.

"No, forty-eight."

"What do you mean?"

"One dollar for the hairdresser—the trip has made my hair filthy, and I must have it washed and set tomorrow morning. Just think how much money you would have saved if we had gone by train!"

Land of
the Future,
Always

THE BOLIVIANS HOLD MANY RECORDS. THEY HAVE THE HIGHEST capital in the world as well as the highest navigable lake, airfield, and skiing grounds. They also use, relatively, more liquor and narcotics and have more illiterates and revolutions than any other South American nation.

But the most surprising thing about Bolivia is its very existence, which seems to disprove the theory of the survival of the fittest, for the Bolivians have lost almost every war they have ever fought. They were beaten by the Chileans who stole their only exit to the sea. They were also whipped by little Paraguay who took a huge bite out of their possessions in the Amazon Valley. It is said that even Queen Victoria once attempted to destroy Bolivia. That was because her ambassador had been treated somewhat undiplomatically. At the order of the Bolivian president he was placed on a donkey, facing the wrong way, and driven through the streets of the capital while the people mocked him.

It was, by the way, his own fault—he had publicly spoken ill of one of the president's mistresses; but that made no difference to Queen Victoria. England, right or wrong! As soon as she heard of the outrage, she sent for the First Lord of the Admiralty.

"Send warships to Bolivia and bombard the capital!" she ordered. The First Lord took out a map of South America and explained that unfortunately it couldn't be done—as Her Majesty could see, Bolivia's capital lay so far from the sea that no guns could reach it.

Queen Victoria grabbed a pencil and crossed out the section of the map which he was pointing at!

"Bolivia," she declared, "no longer exists."

But despite the united efforts of Chile, Paraguay, and the British queen, Bolivia is still the third-largest nation in South America. The country has more than three million inhabitants, and 90 per cent of them are Indians. The first thing a visitor notices is that they are chewing from morning to night. What they munch is the leaves of the coca bush.

"Aha!" I said to myself. "The coca leaf contains cocaine. Cocaine is a narcotic. People love to read about the vices of others—here's something to write about!"

Soon after our arrival I found out that the coca leaves come from Las Yungas, a large province which lies in the Amazon Valley at the foot of the Bolivian plateau. I also discovered that the rainy season had started and that the roads were dangerous. Maybe we had better skip Las Yungas, Chi-yun suggested, adding that I could probably get all the information I needed from the Department of Agriculture. Nothing doing—I was determined to see where the coca leaves grew, and that was that!

We left La Paz, one of the two capitals, at ten o'clock in the morning. An hour later we were in a foggy mountain pass 16,000 feet above sea level. Now we started going downward with screeching brakes. The muddy road ran on the brink of a precipice and was so narrow that two cars couldn't pass without scraping their mudguards. Small wooden crosses marked the spots where careless drivers had fallen down into the abyss. Every time we passed one of these crosses, our driver took off his hat and crossed himself. There were many crosses, and we would have preferred him to keep both hands on the wheel.

At three o'clock we arrived at Las Yungas, 2,000 feet above sea level. I just had time to take a look at a terrace where the coca bushes grew in long, orderly rows. Then the heavens opened their sluices, and local weather prophets predicted that the rain would continue for two weeks. When we returned to La Paz, there were two new crosses along the road and I had learned nothing about coca beyond the fact that it only thrives in a very wet climate.

Now I went to the Department of Agriculture and learned to my joy that it employed no less than two coca specialists. The first one gave me some excellent material. "Coca chewing," he said, "is the curse of Bolivia. It was strictly forbidden under the Incas, but the Spaniards discovered that the Indians could work for longer hours when they chewed the leaves, so they forced them to do it. Today you won't find an Indian who isn't an addict. They're wrecks, physically and mentally. The coca harvest is about six thousand tons a year, after the leaves have been dried. Most of it is consumed locally, the rest exported to Argentina and the States for medical purposes. About 3 per cent of cocaine can be extracted from the leaves. A commission from the antinarcotics department of the United Nations is studying the problem, and Bolivia will probably be requested to make drastic cuts in its coca production."

Very interesting, and all would have been well if I had only kept away from the other specialist. He was a coca enthusiast.

"Haven't you noticed that our Indians have strong, white teeth?" he asked me. "And that they, generally speaking, are very healthy—red cheeks and sparkling eyes? That's because they chew coca. The leaves are chock-full of vitamins. When you live as high up as we do, you need a light stimulant, and the leaves have practically no narcotic effect. A commission from the food department of the United Nations is considering the possibility of purchasing coca from Bolivia and exporting it to the vitamin-starved European nations, perhaps in the form of chewing gum."

What was I to do? I didn't even know for sure whether coca really was a narcotic, so how could I write about it? There seemed to be only one way of finding out—I would have to do some experimenting on my own.

On the way back from the Department of Agriculture I stopped at a grocery store and bought a bag of coca. You can get it anywhere in La Paz; it costs about fifteen cents a pound plus one cent for a handful of baked-ash tablets which are supposed to be chewed simultaneously to bring out the sweet taste of the leaves.

Chi-yun became a bit doubtful when I asked her to try the coca. "I don't want to be a guinea pig," she said. "Why don't you do it yourself?"

I explained what she already knew—that I can't quite

trust myself. By nature I'm an optimist and perpetual enthusiast; if I expect a certain medicine to have a certain effect on me, it invariably does.

She still hesitated. Wouldn't coca stain the teeth? She must be thinking of betel nut, I said—coca would beautify her smile. Hadn't she noticed that all the Indians had strong, white teeth?

Only when I promised to share the experiment with her, did I succeed in persuading her. We stuffed our mouths. The dry leaves crackled between our teeth and had a nasty, bitter taste; the ash tablets didn't help at all. Before long green saliva was dripping down our chins.

"I can feel it!" I exclaimed. "I'm not tired any more!" It was really true. You are always tired in La Paz; there is little oxygen in the air and the town is built on steep hills, but now I felt as if I could sprint up the steepest one of them.

"Imagination!" said Chi-yun, who had only become nauseated from chewing the leaves. I gave her another two mouthfuls, but it still didn't help. Then I asked the servant to brew a large can of coca tea, which we shared. As far as Chi-yun was concerned, it might as well have been water, but I became further intoxicated. Coca, I decided, was much better than opium. Some years before I had smoked a couple of pipes—try everything at least once, is my motto—but they had not had the expected romantic effect. First I wanted to vomit, then I fell asleep and slept like a stone. Coca, on the other hand, gives you a kick—at least it gave me one. I still don't know for sure whether or not it's a strong stimulant. I say yes, Chi-yun says no. I am more inclined to believe her.

But I do know that coca destroys your appetite, and in a way that is a good thing. For many centuries the Bolivian Indians haven't had enough to eat. Don't let the red cheeks fool you. Frequently, the noses are just as red—most of them drink far too much and are undernourished.

How is that possible? There is much rich land in Bolivia: the country should easily be able to feed thirty or forty million people, and there are less than four million. Why, then, don't the Indians get enough to eat?

Strangely enough, because Bolivia is so rich. You can hardly scratch the mountains without finding metal of some kind or another. Before the conquest, the people made their living from agriculture and cattle-raising; the millions of ruined terraces show that they knew how to irrigate. When the Spaniards came, all the Indians were sent down into the mines. The white man was only interested in gold and silver—he drilled down into the earth and neglected its bountiful surface.

Some thirty years ago, a group of foreign agricultural and engineering experts came to Bolivia. They studied the situation carefully and then offered to turn the vast, dry highland into one fertile field. It could easily be done, they said—Lake Titicaca, which lies at the Peruvian border, forms a natural and almost inexhaustible reservoir. The tableland slopes gently down toward Paraguay, and by building dams and digging canals, you could irrigate the entire plateau. If that were done, Bolivia could supply all South America with grain and vegetables—it was only a matter of obtaining the required capital.

Only the mine owners had enough capital for such an undertaking. But they shook their heads. Why should they go to so much trouble? After all, they made a lot of money out of the mines, and it was just as lucrative and much safer to invest their profits abroad.

One would have expected the government to support a project of such vital importance to the whole nation. The government? The Bolivian Republic has existed for almost a century and a quarter, and during that time there have been about one hundred and twenty revolutions. These revolutions were not started by the spark of idealism. Military people are not usually idealistic, and for many, many years the army was apparently the strongest power in the land. The situation resembled that in Peru: behind the army stood the rich—the mine owners—purse in hand. It paid them to be generous to the army, for the soldiers could be relied on to see that the Indian workers behaved. The most important posts were always reserved for obedient officers who lived on a surprisingly grand scale considering their modest salaries.

Sometimes they became jealous of each other. Colonel Juan and his clique thought that Colonel Francisco, the president of the moment, was dividing the cake unfairly. Then Colonel Juan would make a revolution. A couple of soldiers were shot; Francisco moved out of the presidential palace, Juan and his friends moved in. And as soon as they had begun to learn the rudiments of government, Colonel Pedro and his supporters would start another revolution. Some good governments did occasionally come into power, and really try to do something for the country. They might go so far as to draw up plans to establish schools, build roads, and construct canals; they might even get Congress to agree to these plans. Then they were sent packing.

But in 1943-44 a real revolution took place. It was started by a semi-Socialist party which had many supporters among the students and the mestizo middle class in La Paz. When it was all over, the president had been exiled, and some time afterward free elections were held. The Socialists won.

Then a gigantic scheme of social reform was begun. The new government promised the Indians to raise their standard of living to the level of the workers in the United States, and it did pass a number of extremely progressive social laws.

But it is a long jump from the Middle Ages to the twentieth century—Chi-yun and I realized that during a visit to a mine outside La Paz. We were shown around by the manager, and when we came to the living quarters of the workers, he tried to hurry us past them. We stopped, however, and insisted on going inside one of the low, ugly houses.

Each family had one room. The dirt floor seemed to serve as a garbage pail, and the bedstead was a heap of rags in one corner. There were no windows, and the women had to fetch water from a communal well. The mud was several inches deep in the alley which ran between the barracks.

When we returned to the manager, who was waiting for us outside the door, he was red in the face.

"It isn't our fault that the workers live like this," he said. "We've done just about everything we could for them. Two years ago we built several model houses for the workers; I'll show them to you in a little while. They were really nice, with large, bright rooms, running water, modern toilets, and we planned slowly to replace all the barracks with such houses. But you should have seen them a week after the Indians moved in! They cooked in the living room instead of in the kitchen, and cut up the floors to use as firewood. The windows they boarded up—they didn't like the light. They ruined the flush toilets. You see, the Indians up here use stones instead of toilet paper. We tried to teach them not to, but they went on performing their business on the floor and throwing the stones into the toilet bowls.

"We installed shower baths with hot and cold water. They never used them—they're convinced that they'll get pneumonia if they wash themselves. Their wages have doubled in buying power during the last few years. They drink twice as much as before. We have established schools for them, but they won't send their children. We have attempted to make them eat meat and vegetables, but they stick to their old, unhealthy diet of corn, nothing but corn. As long as they can get that and liquor and coca, they're satisfied. It's easy enough for the government to order us to improve the living conditions here, but what can we do when the Indians refuse any kind of improvement?"

Even then it seemed doubtful whether the government would have time to carry out its ambitious social experiment. In La Paz everybody talked about the next revolution. Even members of the government said that it probably wasn't far off, and they were not optimistic about its outcome. Their enemies were not numerous, but they had money and arms. At the moment they were working underground— the Communists, who were trying to buy the support of the Indians with golden promises; the Fascists who probably were backed by the mine owners. Both groups used every opportunity to slander those in power. "The officials steal . . . . ." they whispered. "The government takes bribes . . . . . All the ministers have fortunes salted away outside the country . . . . ."

Some of these accusations were true. Those in power were not angels, but it was the first democratic government which Bolivia had ever had. Since then it has been overthrown. There have been three more revolutions—Bolivia seems to fulfill the sardonic prediction of the Englishman who had spent a number of years in La Paz.

"Bolivia is the land of the future," he said, "and it will always remain the land of the future."

Profiteers or
Benefactors

I sat before a member of the Bolivian Immigration Department who had granted me an interview. He kept glancing at my nose, which ought to have convinced him that his suspicion was unfounded—from the forehead it bends inward, then suddenly takes courage and juts into space.

". . . . if we like the Jews?" The chief repeated my last question and cleared his throat self-consciously. "But *Señor* Eskenstein, aren't you—I mean, didn't you tell me that you live at the Pension Neumann?"

"Yes," I replied, "but I'm Danish and my name is Eske*lund*."

"Ah, Danish!" He smiled. "Then I can speak freely. Sorry about my mistake, but when people live at the Pension Neumann, we usually take for granted that they're refugees. No, we don't like the Jews—we've had very poor experiences with them . . . . ."

212

He began to rattle off a long story which I practically knew by heart, for I had heard it with a few variations in Colombia, Ecuador, and Peru. Until the middle of the thirties there were only a few thousand Jews in South America, the immigration man said. Most of them had come from Spain, and nobody minded them very much because they mixed with the rest of the population and didn't make themselves conspicuous in any way. But after Hitler seized power, a large number of European Jews came to Latin America. At once a Jewish problem arose. By now there were more than a quarter of a million Jews in the countries south of Panama; Bolivia alone had opened its doors to about forty thousand. They had been permitted to come on the condition that they would till the soil; more than 90 per cent of them had entered as farmers or agricultural specialists. Only one Jew had kept his word and taken up farming of a sort: he was employed as a bookkeeper at one of the large plantations.

The rest had settled down in the towns. There were some ten thousand in La Paz, and on the main street one heard as much German as Spanish. The new arrivals stuck together; only very seldom did they marry Bolivians. They came without a cent in their pockets, and today they dominated the business life of the city—they owned the best shops and amusement places and most of the small industries. The Bolivians resented this intrusion. They didn't like to see their native land taken over by a foreign minority. It hurt their national pride. There was no end to the greed of the Jews, and they made themselves ever more hated. . . . . .

As I listened to the immigration man, I thought of the Dane whom I had met a few days before. He was the type of man you instinctively trust, and he had given me a very different picture of the situation.

"When I came to La Paz twelve years ago," he had said, "the town was almost unbearably dull. At ten o'clock the lights went out and the streets were quiet as the grave. There wasn't a single amusement place, not a restaurant where you could get a decent meal. If you wanted to do some shopping, you had to go to Peru or Chile; the stores in La Paz had nothing but a few groceries, homespun Indian cloth, coca, and *aguardiente*. All luxuries had to be imported. You couldn't buy a good suit of clothes.

"Then the Jews came, and things started humming. Don't we have fine shops now? Don't we have excellent night clubs? You ought to buy a new suit here; our tailors make them cheaper and better than anywhere else in South America. No one can help admiring the Jews. They've done a lot for La Paz. The Bolivians won't admit it, of course, but you know—sour grapes."

I know nothing about Jewish business methods in South America, but I do know that the Jews owned the most reasonable hotels and boarding houses along our route, and they always did their most to make us feel at home.

The Pension Neumann, where we stayed in La Paz, was one of the unofficial meeting places for the Jews there. You seldom heard Spanish in the dining room; even the waiters had learned a little German. At all hours of the day, three or four people would be gesticulating and talking loudly at the same time. Their voices cut through the tobacco fumes, and you heard the same word over and over again—Palestine. None of the guests had been there, but the new fatherland was very much in their thoughts.

214

"We're going to Palestine," Mr. Finkenstein would say; he had a small factory and six children. "I want to see my sons and daughters grow up there—they have Bolivian papers, but they'll never become Bolivians. I want them to live in a country which they can really call their own, among their own people."

In another corner Mr. Birnbaum explained why he didn't want to go to Palestine. "I have a good business here," he said, "and I don't like this new Jewish nationalism—it's dangerous. These bands of terrorists—they make me think of the *SS*. . . ."

He ran his hand over his closed eyes. Mr. Birnbaum was an old man and had spent three years in a German concentration camp.

Mr. Goldberg couldn't make up his mind. He wished to die in Palestine, but couldn't persuade himself to leave the business which he had started here. It had taken him four hard years to build it up, and now he was doing well at last.

"Maybe we'll have enough money in a couple of years," he said. "Then we'll go . . . . ."

His wife smiled sadly. She knew that "enough money" was an ever receding goal, that as long as business remained good they would stay in La Paz.

Two of the Jews wanted desperately to get away, but not to Palestine. They had visited the United States en route from Europe and could not forget it. New York—you could make money there, you could buy things with the money! For several years they had waited to get U.S. immigration papers; maybe they would come soon.

One evening, when we were talking about traveling, Mr. Finkenstein asked to see my passport. As he turned over the leaves, the others gathered behind him to read over his shoulder.

"England!" they exclaimed. "The United States, Guatemala, Panama, Mexico!" They looked at me with a mixture of envy and awe. How many countries had I been to? Nearly forty. They shook their heads admiringly. Forty countries! I could just go to any country I chose, ask for a visa, and then I'd get it—wasn't that so? Ah, what wouldn't they give for a Danish passport!

At that moment I understood what Palestine meant to them. For so many years they had been "stateless." They had been kicked out of Europe and into what they considered a prison—Bolivia, the only country which would accept them. They longed to escape from it, and Palestine was the key to their cell door.

When the conversation became too loud, an irritated "Shhh!" would come from the corner where the poker players sat. Even with unusually bad luck one could not lose more than four or five dollars, but they played as if their lives were at stake. The losers would slap their foreheads and groan, while the winners smiled from ear to ear. Sometimes a player would cogitate for several minutes when his turn came, but in the end he almost invariably threw his chip into the pot—even if he held nothing, he couldn't resist the chance of winning a dollar for five cents. The game had very little in common with poker; you just sat around and waited to get the highest hand. But they had a lot of fun, and so did I.

We arrived in La Paz in the middle of December, and planned to leave for Chile on Christmas Eve. But Mrs. Goldberg wouldn't hear of it.

"I know how lonely Christmas Eve can be when you're in a strange country," she said. "You come home with us— we're not having a big party, but at least it'll be better than spending Christmas on the train."

About seven in the evening they came to fetch us. Their three-room apartment smelled of burning pine needles. In the sitting room there was a large Christmas tree which Mrs. Goldberg had decorated with cotton wool and silver paper. The candlesticks she had made out of clothespins.

"We're not Christians, but we always celebrate Christmas the way we did in Germany," she said. "Sit down—we're expecting two more guests, old friends from Germany. I do hope you'll like the food."

While we were eating the excellent German meal, Mr. Goldberg told us about the first difficult years in Bolivia. When he and his wife arrived in 1940, they had shared a small hotel room with another Jewish family. It was impossible to get any work; they pawned everything they owned and lived on bread and goat cheese. Whenever they left the room, the owner would come running with the bill.

After several months Mr. Goldberg had finally found a job as a dishwasher in a restaurant. The pay was less than twenty-five dollars a month, but he could fill his pockets with food which he brought home to the others. Two weeks later he was offered a job at a garage, and took it though he knew nothing about cars. From six in the evening until two in the morning he washed dishes, and at 6:00 A.M. he began working at the garage. Twice he was nearly fired for falling asleep beneath cars which he was supposed to be repairing. "He regained the slenderness of his youth," Mrs. Goldberg put in.

When he had saved a little money, he rented a shed on the outskirts of the town, bought a secondhand washing machine and a couple of irons, and he and his wife began to take in washing. A year later they sold the laundry for five times what they had paid for it. Mr. Goldberg went into partnership with another man and became a leather manufacturer; now their factory employed more than sixty workers.

"Yes, we have a lot to be grateful for," said Mrs. Goldberg. "There were many others who were not so lucky."

I knew what she was thinking of. Mr. Goldberg had told us that her brother and her parents had disappeared during the war.

When we had finished eating, she lit the candles on the tree. Mr. Stein, the old friend from Berlin, began to sing *"Stille Nacht, heilige Nacht."* We all joined in, Chi-yun in English and I in Danish. The three languages sounded almost like one, and not since I was a boy had I been in such a solemn mood on Christmas Eve—but then I had drunk a whole bottle of Chilean white wine before dinner.

Mrs. Stein distributed the presents. There was nothing for me, I knew—Chi-yun *had* bought a present for me, but I had spoiled the fun by finding it the day before. It wasn't my fault, really: I was in our hotel bedroom trying to write an article about the Incas, when suddenly I began to sniff. What was that smell? I lit a cigarette and went on working, but a few minutes later the stench again called my thoughts away from the Inca empire. Then I started to search in earnest—there must be a dead rat somewhere in the room. Guided by my sense of smell, I went to the writing desk and opened one drawer after another. The first three yielded nothing, but in the fourth I found a small, white parcel containing a quarter of a pound of my favorite cheese, Camembert.

When Chi-yun returned, as soon as our eyes met, we both burst out laughing.

"So you found it!" she said. "They refused to keep it in the kitchen, and judging by the smell it won't keep till tomorrow—we'd better eat it right away."

Her present from me, a gold bracelet, she had received several weeks before. So we sat down in a corner and listened to the happy exclamations from the others as they opened their presents. Our thoughts returned to Guatemala—perhaps Mei-mei and Father were also opening presents at that moment. It was her first Christmas without us.

"Mr. Eskelund . . . . ." Mrs. Stein handed me a large package. "And Mrs. Eskelund." Chi-yun got three! The Goldbergs and the Steins had bought two pounds of chocolate, a silver bracelet, and a pair of silver earrings for her. I was given an awe-inspiring Bolivian Devil's mask with long horns and glass teeth.

At midnight the many church bells of the city began to ring. "Now we'll show you how the Indians celebrate Christmas," said Mr. Goldberg. We went out to the main plaza, and as soon as we reached it, a hollow booming began to mingle with the bells. It grew ever louder until it almost drowned the sound from the churches; and then a burning snake appeared on the dark main street. In front staggered four Indians who were hammering away on big drums, and behind them writhed the snake—a long file of Indians with flaming torches held above their heads. Distorted faces glistened in the light, and the *aguardiente* could be smelled many feet away. I saw a young woman with a child tied to her back; she reeled over to one of the men, tore a bottle of firewater from him, and drank most of it before he could get it back.

Now the church bells stopped ringing, but the drums went on. Down the side streets came other processions of Indians. Even while drinking, they continued to dance; their legs seemed to move mechanically. Many of them collapsed in the streets, and only toward morning was there silence in the city.

On the third day after Christmas we left La Paz. The Goldbergs had invited us to spend New Year's Eve with them, but we wanted to go to Viña del Mar, the famous Chilean resort. Two groaning locomotives pulled the train out of the deep basin at the bottom of which lies the Bolivian capital. For a day and a half we rolled across the monotonous highland of the Andes. Occasionally a lake would appear—we could see the waves, almost feel the fresh wind, but a second later the mirage would be swallowed up by the dry desert.

It was night when we arrived at Antofagasta, the main port of northern Chile. The town is famous for its delicious scallops and its picturesque situation at the foot of a steep mountain. We had to extract this information from a guidebook, however, for at daybreak we climbed into an airplane. The morning haze had drawn a thick veil over Antofagasta; all we could see was a mountain peak and the Pacific.

Four hours later we landed in Santiago. It was midsummer down here, and after an intolerably hot night in the capital we fled to Viña del Mar. This residential town couldn't have a more suitable name. It is almost too beautiful—it reminds one of a colored post card, and the words turn honey-sweet in my mouth when I try to describe it.

Its pride is the Casino. Here the elite of South America meet—business tycoons from Brazil, kings of Argentinian cattle empires, accompanied by their wives or mistresses. New Year's Eve is the biggest social event of the year, and the white marble building was crowded to capacity when Chi-yun and I entered it an hour before midnight. For a while we amused ourselves by trying to guess which numbers would win on the roulette wheels. It was fun, for we lost all the time. A few minutes before twelve people left the gambling tables and streamed toward the vast ballroom. We followed the current, but got no further than the door when a waiter stopped me—sorry, *Señor,* but only men in evening dress are permitted to enter . . . . .

I got furious and tried to force my way past him, but two other waiters rushed to his aid. This had a quietening effect on me, and I let Chi-yun persuade me to accompany her into the reading room on the second floor. Here we greeted the New Year among dusty books and dog-eared weeklies. Downstairs the orchestra played, champagne corks popped, and we thought sadly of how pleasant the evening would have been if we had only stayed with our Jewish friends in La Paz.

Chile's New Look

MOST PEOPLE IN VALPARAÍSO KNOW THE STERN OLD GENTLEMAN by sight. They also recognize the wheezy horn of his ancient car—bicycles and other cars dash to the right when they hear it, even the trams slow down, and pedestrians look about them carefully before they cross the street.

Despite these precautions it frequently happens that his Ford bumps into another car, for the old man ignores the traffic lights. Sometimes the owner of a damaged car will become furious and demand compensation, but that's only because he does not know with whom he is dealing. He is soon told when a policeman comes on the scene.

"Don't you know who he is?" the policeman will ask with a respectful nod toward the old man. "That's the Danish doctor from the children's hospital. Yes, I know it was his fault, but we couldn't possibly bring a charge against *him*."

And the old man is allowed to drive on. When he arrives home, the gardner waits outside the garage with a brush and a pot of paint. There are usually a few scratches which have to be painted over, and sometimes the doctor himself needs to be patched up a bit, too. He is undoubtedly the worst driver in Valparaíso; many consider him a public danger. But he is also an honorary citizen of the town and its leading public benefactor.

I won't say that the people of Valparaíso love him. He's too remote and silent for that, but they look up to him, they idolize him. When he dies, some will probably worship him as a kind of saint, though it is doubtful whether he can be called a god-fearing man himself. He never goes to church —in his opinion, you should practice Christianity throughout the week and not just on Sunday mornings. This he has done, and some two hundred thousand people can bear witness to it.

Only a few can remember the day he arrived at Valparaíso, for it is now fifty-four years ago. I have seen a photograph of him from that time—a tall, bony young man with blond hair, an aquiline nose, and an unusually broad and prominent forehead. He was then twenty-seven and had just received his medical degree. His gentle little wife smiles nervously in the picture; Dr. John Thierry stares brusquely into the camera as if to say: "Please get it over quickly—I have no time for such nonsense."

Fifty-five days after his arrival in Valparaíso, the second largest city in Chile, he had to pass another medical examination, this time in Spanish. The young Dane got the highest grade out of more than twenty candidates.

"Well, I had spent nearly two months in the country by then," Dr. Thierry says. "So I'd had plenty of time to learn the language."

He was an eye specialist and soon developed a good practice. It seemed wrong to him, however, that he was to work only for the few who could afford to pay. On his way to and from the clinic where he worked, he saw many sick people, and his long, strong doctor's hands itched to heal them. One day he spoke to his wife about it.

"Of course we can't help them all," he said. "There are too many—but we can do something for the children."

Dr. Thierry does nothing half-heartedly, and he never listens to others. If his conscience says this is right, then it is right even if the whole world says the opposite. Many call him an egocentric, and so he is, but he never thinks of himself.

Everybody raised objections when he suggested founding a clinic for children. Such a thing ought to be left to the Catholic charitable organizations—the Church would become jealous if a Protestant reaped the honor of starting a project which was bound to become popular among the poor.

Dr. Thierry did not care a hang for the honor; he has a large collection of decorations lying at the bottom of his chest of drawers and would probably be glad to exchange them for a new pipe. He has an impressive number of old grandfather pipes; most of them are cracked and leaky, but he will not part with them and constantly repairs them with tape and glue. A good pipe of tobacco is one of his greatest pleasures, but once he stopped smoking for twenty years. He had no special reason for doing so—"I just wanted to prove to myself that I had the will power," he explains.

The children's clinic was the first one of its kind in Chile, and today it is the largest and the best in the country.

It is really no longer a clinic, but a hospital with sixty beds, ten doctors, and thirty nurses. Since it was started, more than two hundred thousand children have been treated without any cost to their parents.

When we visited the hospital, the waiting room was crowded with mothers carrying sick children. One by one they were shown in to the doctors. The fear had left their eyes when they came out again, and I thought of all the mothers who in the course of the years had passed through those doors—even with a table of logarithms you couldn't calculate their gratitude.

When we had waited for a while, I was shown into Dr. Thierry's office. He was treating a three-year-old for rash.

"So you're a journalist," he said, swabbing the swollen arms of the child with some kind of medicine. "I just want to tell you not to forget Miss Tvede if you write about the hospital. She has been the driving spirit—she and my wife have done the real work."

The child had been crying when I entered. Now it was smiling confidently at Dr. Thierry, why I don't know, for in his white gown he looked forbidding, almost awe-inspiring.

"Well, that was all I wanted to say." Dr. Thierry cleared his throat. "Good morning, young man."

"My wife is outside," I said. "Her earlobes are badly inflamed—would you mind having a look at them?"

"Not at all." He greeted Chi-yun kindly and examined the holes pierced by *Tia* Bates's cook in Arequipa—they were full of pus; the needle probably hadn't been clean. Dr. Thierry turned a pair of accusing gray eyes at my wife.

"Little girls can't help it if their parents disfigure them like this," he said. "But why a grown-up woman should want to do it of her own free will is beyond my comprehension."

He swabbed the earlobes with iodine and sent for the next patient.

A moment later we met the chief nurse, a thin, gray woman. During her thirty years at the hospital, she has often wondered why the children reach out for her when she walks through the wards. Nature gave her untiring energy and a warm heart, but did not go to much trouble about her looks. Kamma Tvede calls herself ugly. She says it with a smile, and it is this smile which makes the children love her.

You feel almost embarrassed when you hear her talk of Dr. Thierry. She worships him; I think that she would willingly sacrifice her life for him and be thankful to do so. For hours she can talk about how the doctor acted in some emergency, how he saved the little boy with pneumonia when all the other doctors had given him up. She moves her hands as she speaks, blinks nervously, becomes more and more tense. Work gives her vitality a more natural outlet than words. Apart from managing the hospital, she has trained more than 10 per cent of Chile's two thousand nurses. When I began to question her about herself, she became suspicious. Why did I want to know these things? Because I wanted to write about her.

"Silly!" she said. "I'm not worth writing about, I've only been—how shall I put it?—one of Dr. Thierry's instruments. He's been so patient with me! When he leaves us"—her face contracted—"the hospital won't be the same any more. Just the sight of him gives us courage, and I can assure you that it hasn't always been easy. We exist on charity, and often we don't know how we're going to get food and salaries for the coming week. But we always manage somehow . . . . . Do you know whom you ought to write about, I mean, apart from Dr. Thierry? Mrs. Thierry! She has administered the hospital ever since it was founded—she's the one who has made both ends meet, and it has been a thankless task."

When I went to see Mrs. Thierry, a mild, fragile lady with snow-white hair, she denied having contributed anything toward the success of the hospital. Her husband and Kamma Tvede had done all the real work—she had only helped by raising funds and keeping the accounts straight. Spare-time work, nothing more—after all, she'd had their two daughters to bring up.

Never before had Chile seen anything like the way Dr. Thierry brought up his daughters. Before they were born, he had read a book on child education. He is a systematic man and it was a conservative book. The two little girls had their fair heads shaven, for the sake of cleanliness; only at the age of ten were they allowed to have crew-cuts. They wore sailor suits; that was most practical. Dr. Thierry himself wears the same kind of clothes all the year round: black suit and a white shirt with starched collar. Whether it's cold winter or hot summer makes no difference; he just doesn't notice the temperature.

The two girls were laughed at in school, but it never even occurred to them to ask their father for permission to grow their hair long or to dress like the other children. His word was law, and they had been taught to obey. The teachers were not fond of them, for even when it poured, their father would send them to school. All the other children stayed at home when it rained, and the poor teachers were forced to keep the school open merely for the sake of the daughters of the righteous Dane.

The other children would often ask them questions about their father. "He never goes to church," they said. "Is it really true that he is a heathen?"

"We don't know," Dr. Thierry's daughters answered. "We only know that he says: 'Do better unto others than you would unto yourself.'"

He set aside a certain number of hours a day for the children to do their homework. They were never permitted to go out in the evenings. Word by word, the doctor followed the advice of the book on child education. It must have stopped with the legal age, for when his elder daughter became eighteen she was suddenly allowed to do anything she wanted. She was then studying at a boarding school in the capital, and a week after her birthday Dr. Thierry received an angry letter from the principal. *Señorita* Thierry's behavior was scandalous, he wrote—she had suddenly begun to use powder and lipstick, and she stayed out until after midnight!

"*Señorita* Thierry is now a grown-up lady," the doctor answered in a frigid letter, "and as such she is permitted to follow her own inclinations.'

To call Dr. Thierry's way of life original is no exaggeration. He never goes to bed until 2:00 A.M., and the hours between dinner and bedtime he spends with a book and a pipe. Scientific literature is his favorite fare; for diversion he reads the classics in Greek and Latin. When he falls ill, he refuses to swallow as much as a teaspoonful of the medicine which he daily prescribes to his patients. Instead he pulls down the blinds, goes to bed, and refuses to eat or talk. Sometimes three or four days pass before he is well again. If he has an aching tooth, he pulls it out himself without an anesthetic.

For many years he had a summer house near a treacherous river in southern Chile. People said that the river was unnavigable. Dr. Thierry said no. He considered the problem for a long time and finally built a boat which looked like a large bathtub. The whole family as well as the neighbors gathered on the bank to watch the maiden voyage. The doctor launched the boat singlehanded, started the engine, and waved his pipe.

The boat couldn't turn over, he said, and it didn't. It sank like a stone. Dr. Thierry floated off with the current, still puffing at his pipe. It was still burning when he waded ashore at a point further down river. During his next summer holiday he built another boat, and if it had also sunk he would have built still another. Fortunately, it stayed afloat.

Not far from the summer house was a lake where the family went bathing. Once Dr. Thierry dropped his glasses off a pier. He is farsighted and insisted that he could see them down at the bottom of the lake. The water was deep, however, and though a good diver the doctor could not reach the bottom. After much deliberation he took a large stone, tied it round his neck, and dived again. This time he did reach the shiny object, which proved to be an empty sardine can.

When Dr. Thierry became sixty-one, he decided that he wanted a car, so he bought the old Ford and, he claims, taught himself to drive. His family denies that he has ever learned it. That is an exaggeration. He can start the car, and he is not bad at steering, but he is very absent-minded and fails to notice others in the street. No one knows exactly how many accidents he has had; one of his daughters told me that the total must be in four figures. He has ceased offering lifts to people, for they always refuse.

Once he even managed to drive over himself! He had parked his car on a hill and it refused to start. No one knows for certain how it happened, but after many useless attempts with the self-starter, Dr. Thierry got out and began pulling at the front bumper. Then suddenly the car made up its mind to go, and the doctor got a bad gash in his head. It took three weeks to repair the Ford. Dr. Thierry walked home. He has never taken a taxi; it is against his principles.

During one of my conversations with him I said: "Dr. Thierry, do you believe——"

"No, I don't," he interrupted. "There are certain things I know and many more things I don't know."

He does know that religion and politics usually go hand-in-hand in Latin America. Never has he permitted the Church or the politicians to have anything to do with his hospital, and people admire him for it. Governments have fallen, dictatorial presidents have been deposed, the Church has had its ups and downs, but Dr. Thierry is still there—not quite as erect as before, for he is over eighty now, but as untiring as ever in his efforts to help those who cannot help themselves.

And there are many who can't, even though Chile in most respects is a surprisingly advanced country. When you arrive there from the north, you can hardly believe that you are still in Latin America. The country is much cleaner than its neighbors along the Pacific and has much less class distinction. There are rich and poor—there always will be as long as some are energetic, others lazy—but they are not separated by a chasm, only by a small valley. People are not so distrustful of each other—you discover that when you take your first bus ride. In the other Latin American countries which we had passed through, one man drives the bus, another sells the tickets, and every few minutes an inspector jumps on to make sure that there is no monkey business. In Chile the driver is also the ticket seller and the controller, and the service is much better.

The country is more than three thousand miles long and has been compared to a worm with its tail in ice water, its head in fire. Southern Chile is as thinly populated as Nevada, for down there the climate is raw and stormy all year round. Sheep thrive fairly well, and nothing much else. When Charles Darwin visited Tierra del Fuego in 1834, he was not impressed by the natives. The young scientist wrote in his diary that the visiting Englishmen nearly went mad from listening to the constant yells of the natives, who were dressed in stinking sheepskin and stole everything they could lay their hands on. "Yammerschooner, yammerschooner!" they would shout endlessly—give me something, give me something!

A native girl was selected and brought to England to learn about British culture. During her stay in London, the King gave her an audience and chucked her under the chin. Three years later she was sent back to Tierra del Fuego to enlighten her countrymen. The first thing she did was to open a shop with herself as the only commodity.

231

Northern Chile is even more desolate. Here lies a dry, hot desert, barren and yet rich in a material which can either benefit humanity or hasten its destruction. It depends on the use you make of the nitrate. It's about to go out of fashion, however—you can make it from air, and much more effective explosives than mere dynamite have been developed.

In Central Chile live nearly 90 per cent of the country's six million inhabitants. The climate is somewhat like that of Italy, and the heart of Chile reminds one of the long Mediterranean peninsula. Volcanoes send their hot breath toward the blue sky, oxen pull the plows through the rich soil, and the people drink wine and smile easily. The food is excellent, and in a way we have the Spaniards to thank for this. They are not good cooks, but their narrow colonial policy brought French methods to the country.

Spain had prohibited trade among her possessions in the new world; only ships which came directly from the mother country were allowed to enter the harbors. Chile had neither gold nor silver to tempt the Spanish schooners, and sometimes months would pass without the arrival of a ship with supplies from Spain. French smugglers decided that this was most unjust. Before long a lively trade was taking place between France and the isolated colonists; it was not uncommon to see a dozen French ships lying at anchor off Valparaíso. The townspeople were often invited to meals on board, and the Frenchmen gave them the very best which their cooks could provide. The Spanish *señoras* soon realized that the food was far superior to their own unimaginative dishes. They copied the recipes, which henceforth were handed down from mothers to daughters, so that even today you find that the food in Chile is nearly as good as that in France.

One of the first Spanish noblemen to arrive in Central Chile was Pedro de Valdivia. His opinion of the country we know from a letter which he wrote to King Charles V in 1554:

. . . . . Your Majesty can inform the merchants and the people who desire to emigrate that there is no better place in the world than here for settling down. This I say because it is flat, very healthy and very appealing country, with short winters, and only when there is a quarter-moon does it rain for a day or two, and on all other days of the year the sun shines so warmly that it is not necessary to light a fire . . . . . There is a wealth of meadows and fields where every type of plant and animal can find nourishment, and a wealth of trees for building houses . . . . It seems indeed as if the Good Lord has made this land merely to hold it out in the hollow of his hand and show us the wonders he can create . . . . .

Valdivia did not exaggerate, but he forgot that all these wonders already belonged to another people: the Araucans. These hardy Indians were not eager to let themselves be pushed out of the hollow of God's hand. They had kept the Incas at bay and were to give the Spaniards more gray hairs than any other people in South America. The redskins in the United States were children playing at war in comparison. It took the Spaniards nearly three hundred years to subdue the Araucans.

Valdivia himself fell in the struggle. At the head of a large Spanish force he rode into the dense forest toward the east to punish the Indians for raiding a Spanish settlement. It would be an easy matter to teach the Araucans a lesson, the conquerors thought; after all, they were on horseback, and the clubs and arrows of the Araucans were no match for modern firearms.

As Valdivia rode through the forest he probably gave no thought to his former stableboy Lautaro, who two or three years before had run off with some of the commandant's horses. He was tall for an Araucan, broad-shouldered, and had flashing black eyes.

The attack came without warning, and it wasn't a band of howling barbarians who hurled themselves at the punitive expedition. The Indians were on horseback! And they, too, had firearms!

In the history of the conquest we read page after page about the incredible courage of the Spaniards. They *were* brave men, but they had great advantages. In the forest of Central Chile, they faced the Indians for the first time on equal terms. The Spaniards suffered an ignominious defeat. Valdivia himself was made prisoner and, mortally wounded, was taken before the Indian commander-in-chief, who proved to be none other than Lautaro, his former stableboy —it was he who had organized the Indians, and had taught them to ride and use firearms.

Lautaro's name lived long after his death. You can see his statue in Temuco, a poor little provincial town which was once the center of Araucan resistance. Proud and defiant he looks toward the north where the enemy was entrenched, but the statue is only a dead symbol. In 1861 the last battle took place between the Indians and the forces of republican Chile. The Araucans were defeated, and it was as if their desire to live ceased at that moment.

They were not oppressed or maltreated. The government gave each one a small piece of land—a noble gesture, but it was not enough. The Araucan is not suited to being fenced in and to raising corn. Take the wild forest away from him, and he is lost. Today there are hardly fifty thousand Araucans left; in a hundred years there probably will not be five hundred. There can be no compromise in the struggle between the children of nature and those of the modern world, and it is always the former who lose. We sell them an anesthetic—alcohol—so their death is relatively painless.

Some say that Chile has progressed so much lately because there are practically no Indians in the country. I think it is due to another reason. The constant fighting against the Araucans toughened the whites in Chile. There was no gold, so it was not the greedy adventurer who came, but the hard-working farmer. Many of the immigrants were Irish, Basque, and German. If they had had slaves, they would probably have developed the same mentality as the Spaniards in Bolivia, Peru, and Ecuador. But the Araucan was no man's thrall—the Europeans had to do their own work and thus never had a chance to become lazy and useless. The lower classes were white and wouldn't stand being kicked around.

Not that there was not some kicking around in the beginning. For many years the upper classes were in power, but in 1932 the strong progressive forces won a clear-cut victory, and since then the country has kept to a healthy middle-of-the-road course, with only a few lapses.

If you ask a native what Chile needs most of all, chances are he'll answer "capital." There are few factories in the country, so Chile must import most of its industrial goods from Argentina and the United States. This annoys the Chileans, who do not like to be dependent on the great powers. They are also extremely conscious of the fact that all the large copper mines in the country are in American and British hands. When the Chileans asked for loans to develop new industries in their country, they were usually told: "Why should we help you to establish factories which will compete with our own? If you want to borrow money, you must give us concessions."

Recently, however, Chile did get large loans on a fair basis from several United States firms and from the World Bank. Most of the money was used to build a steel plant which will be the second or third largest in Latin America.

"Once we're making our own steel, our industrial revolution will begin in earnest," the Chileans say. "Our possibilities are practically unlimited—maybe we'll even begin to export industrial products one of these days."

Yes, why not? Chile is a strong, progressive nation, extremely pleasant to visit, for it has not been infected by the chauvinism of its neighbors. It's true that the Chileans often make fun of the Anglo-Saxons.

"They only come here to make money," they say. "As soon as they've filled their pockets, they go away, and all they leave behind them is holes in the ground."

But the Americans and the British are really very popular in Chile, especially among the girls. I discovered this while collecting material for an article on Chilean women. For two days I strolled about on the beaches of Viña del Mar, followed by Chi-yun, who kept at a discreet distance. Whenever I saw a really beautiful girl I would go over and ask permission to photograph her. She did not mind that, nor being interviewed afterward. Invariably she would ask where I came from. "Oh!" she would say, disappointed when I answered *Dinamarca*. "And I thought you were a Yankee!"

To be married to a Yankee was the young women's great ambition. If not a Yankee, then an Englishman, and if not that, someone from elsewhere in Europe. Foreign men were *so* much nicer than the Latins, they said.

They smiled sweetly at me, the foreigner, and I purred like a kitten having its back scratched—until I happened to remember Chi-yun who was probably sitting down somewhere nearby. I could not very well let her wait indefinitely, so I called to her to come over.

It was pitiful to watch the change in the bathing beauties when I said, "I'd like to introduce my wife." From that moment they would not waste another glance on me.

Surprise
for Mei-mei

WE HAD INTENDED TO WIND UP THE TRIP AT CAPE HORN, BUT during the last two months a little girl with thin legs and big, brown eyes had pursued us in our dreams, and we could not forget her when we awoke. Now, far down in southern Chile, our longing to see her became stronger than anything else. We agreed that the natives of Tierra del Fuego could do very well without us, while we could no longer do without Mei-mei. We wanted to go home.

On the "Flecha del Sur"—the impressive name of Chile's southern express train—we rumbled back to Valparaíso. Three days later we were on our way to Panama aboard an Italian steamer. The tickets were as cheap as the food was poor—we paid $180 for the two of us and got nothing to eat but badly cooked spaghetti, macaroni, and rolls without butter.

From Panamá we flew to Guatemala. The minutes grew longer and longer as the hour of reunion approached. The customs inspection in Guatemala City was the most exasperating we had experienced. All our things were taken out of our suitcases—we had bought an extra one in Peru to have room for all our belongings—and put on the counter. It was a colorful sight: three pairs of shoes which Chi-yun had bought in Chile, four Chinese dresses from Lima, twenty-odd, silver ornaments from Arequipa, four handbags and a suit which I had bought in La Paz, two dolls, a paintbox and a Spanish ABC for Mei-mei, six cans of Chilean lobster, and three pounds of candied fruit. All this included, the six-month trip had cost us just under two thousand dollars.

When the suitcases were empty, the customs inspector looked questioningly at our bulging overcoats.

"And what have you got in your pockets?" he asked.

In our pockets? Hm!

We had smuggled our little Indian family—husband, wife, and son—across many frontiers by now. Had all our efforts been in vain? Would our precious tsantsas be confiscated—would we be caught red-handed here on the very threshold of our home? It seemed ironic, devilish, but there was no escape. We pulled out the heads. I closed my eyes, expecting the worst—then I heard Chi-yun's voice.

"They're for our daughter," she said brightly. "Dolls from Ecuador!"

"Dolls? They look almost human—like dwarf heads!" The customs man smiled at his own joke, and we broke into rather forced laughter. "But you have no American cigarettes?" he continued. "Well, as far as I can see there's nothing dutiable except the lobsters, but that's so little. . . . ."

We took the first bus to the lake, and when we saw it again—our sapphire-blue Lago de Atitlan surrounded by rugged volcanoes—we agreed that nowhere else had we seen anything so beautiful. We got two Indians to carry our suitcases, and then ran all the way to the bungalow. The pink roses were in bloom; underneath the big fir tree sat my father, carving a wooden figure. He rose and shook hands with us.

"Mei-mei is at Mango's," he said. "I'll go and get her."

"We'll hide in the bedroom," I said. "Don't tell her that we're here—just say you have a surprise for her."

A moment later we could hear Mei-mei's excited voice as she entered the bungalow, two inches taller than when we had left and with a brand new front tooth.

"Hello, Daddy and Mamma!" she shouted, embracing us. Then she looked up at my father.

"But, Farfar," she said, "where's the surprise?"

Printed in U.S.A.

Caribbean Sea

Guatemala City

Barranquilla

VENEZUELA

Panamá

Bogotá

COLOMBIA

ECUADOR

N

Equator

Tumbes

P E R U

Machu
Picchu
Cusco

Lima

CHINCHA
ISLAND

Arequipa

B

Vagabond
Fever

The Eskelunds' Route
by Air and Land ━━━➤
Their Route by Water ━ ━ ━

Pacific Ocean